Trailside Shelters

Skye Davis

Illustrated by Russ Mohney

STACKPOLE BOOKS

TRAILSIDE SHELTERS
Copyright © 1977 by
Russ Mohney

Published by
STACKPOLE BOOKS
Cameron and Kelker Streets
P.O. Box 1831
Harrisburg, Pa. 17105

Published simultaneously in Don Mills, Ontario, Canada by
Thomas Nelson & Sons, Ltd.

Printed in the U.S.A.

Library of Congress Cataloging in Publication Data

Skye Davis.
    Trailside shelters.

    Includes index.
    1. Camping—Outfits, supplies, etc.—Catalogs.
2. Tents—Catalogs.   I. Title.
GV191.76.M63   1977   685′.53   77-21610
ISBN 0-8117-2268-6

To my mother, who made our place in tents and shanties when times were poor; and who taught us with grace and good cheer that a home is neither wood nor stone, but rather a circle of light in the darkness.

The years have moved us into more substantial dwellings, but her unfailing example has given us spirits as free and uncluttered as those early places—and souls at peace with the wilderness.

Contents

Preface

When one sets about to write at length about such a primitive and simple device as the common tent (and they are much more common now than a generation ago), it would seem the subject would soon be exhausted. Such, however, is not the case.

The tent, the most primitive of manufactured shelters, is a great deal more than a few yards of cloth or canvas and a shank of braided line. The modern development of material and design notwithstanding, the tent is a specter that has intrigued each of us from infancy, fascinated us collectively since the dawn of time. So, you see, it is less the tent that we write about than the spiritual experience it so uniquely represents.

Every season an increasing number of us cast off—for a few days at least—the encumbrance of a pressurized society and seek our recreation in the vastness of the wilderness. Unfailingly, the tattered little tent is the center of our occupation, the focal point

of the adventure. More objectively, its aura of familiarity in a foreign environment becomes our goal; the
tent represents the last umbilical tie with a more
domestic existence. Few travelers in the outdoors
would admit to such an intimate relationship with their
little canvas shelter, but the same hiker who replaces
his boots as an annual matter balks at changing tents
so long as a few threads hold it together. It isn't
surprising!

If the nomad of antiquity held strong feelings for his
somewhat mobile dwelling, that love affair has only
intensified in the centuries that followed. No person
with more than a casual acquaintance with the wilderness would venture out without his tent, experience
being the factor that keeps him in such close communi-
cation with his shelter. Although birchbark and buffalo
hides have given way to nylon and netting, the tent is
still an island of comfort on the changing face of the
wilderness. That tiny twinge of affection, though pre-
dicated on comfort and safety, is rooted deep in his
past. With his usual penetrating accuracy, Thoreau
once observed:

> Who does not remember the interest with which when
> young he looked at shelving rocks, or any approach to
> a cave? It was the natural yearning of that portion of
> our most primitive ancestor which still survived in us.
> From the cave we have advanced to roofs of palm
> leaves, of bark and boughs, of linen woven and
> stretched, of grass and straw, of stones and tiles. At
> last, we know not what it is to live in the open air, and
> our lives are more domestic in more senses than we
> think.

From a purely practical point of view, the simple
tent is probably the only kind of shelter that allows us
to roam where we will and still maintain the regular
routine of "housekeeping" that we have come to de-

mand of ourselves. Perhaps we would be happier, as a whole, if we were to adopt the tent as our everyday dwelling, rejecting a neighborhood when it no longer suited us, seeking out instead a place of peace and beauty. However implausible such a way of life may be, it *is* possible to live in a tent for a short time and then bring a spirit of freedom and flexibility back into the real world with us. As a realizable goal, that is precisely what hundreds of thousands of people are now trying to do with their annual outings.

In the pages that follow we will not only investigate the modern tent from a physical standpoint, attempting to determine just what a particular model or design can do for us, but we will deal with those things quite beyond our tent or our control. It is quite true that the hiker and camper looks to the tent as a visible sign of security and a place of comfort. It is likewise true that the tent alone cannot provide these things. It is the skill and attitude of the camper that is most responsible for securing the desired results.

Thus, we have carefully outlined the complexities of a vast array of tents and shelters, knowing that one of them can provide the opportunity for anyone to enjoy rich and rewarding outdoor experience. Realizing that the accessories—both physical and spiritual—will finally determine the depth of the experience, we've tried to tuck those in, too!

CHAPTER 1

The Moveable Mansion

The self-propelled wanderer of today has a unique opportunity to experience one of mankind's oldest pleasures—stopping during a hike, erecting his* portable shelter, and thereby acquiring a place of his own in the wilderness. It is a temporary home at best, but it still represents a place of relative peace and familiarity that can be enjoyed just as long as he chooses.

HISTORY OF THE TENT

Despite the transient nature of the tent, it is a stable and utterly efficient means of protection against the elements. Tents have been—and still are—used in vir-

---

Note: Throughout this book you will find wide use of such words as "he," "him," and "man." This group of terms has been used only for convenience of explanation or to correspond to manufacturers' designations. Except where specifically noted, they are used in the generic sense and actually denote the human race as a whole.

tually every environment on earth. The early explorer
was no more surprised to see a tent pitched on the arid
sand of the Sahara than he was to visit another snug-
gled among the hummocks of the frozen Arctic. In one
form or another, the tent was the domestic mainstay of
societies all over the earth.

We can only speculate that the tent was independently developed by dozens of diverse societies,
but we can be certain that it was eventually adapted by
each of those early cultures to meet the specific requirements of their own environs. That is, incidentally, precisely the same guide that should be used
by the modern recreational camper in selecting his
particular shelter. The adaptations were truly
remarkable; the tepee of the Plains Indians, for
example, was absolutely suited to the nomadic culture
it served. It was an ideal shelter against the incessant
winds of the prairies, designed to shed the winter rains
and snows with great efficiency. The tepee had a
clever opening at the top to allow smoke to escape, yet
could be closed during periods of foul weather. That
arrangement was remarkably practical; it prevented
the prairie breezes from carrying the fire's heat away
from the pot, making outdoor cooking virtually impossible. If there was a drawback to this unique early
shelter, it was the requirement for a dozen or more
slender poles needed to support it. Long lodgepoles,
often fourteen feet or more in length, were scarce on
the rolling prairielands; so each band had to carry the
poles along on every move. It wasn't long before they
had developed a system by which the poles were
dragged behind the horses, the skin tent folded on top,
and the family fortune tucked among the folds. The
tepee served not only as a shelter, but as the means by
which everything else was transported.

The tepee was one of the most practical shelters ever devised, and remains so today. It is an impossible device for the modern hiker or backpacker, particularly since poles may not be cut in most areas (and shouldn't be chopped for shelter anywhere!), but the design remains one of remarkable efficiency. In some areas of North America devoted to alternative lifestyles, the tepee is making an astonishing comeback.

Equally efficient for its demanding environment was the shallow skin tent of the northern Indians and Eskimos. Contrary to the modern image of these hardy peoples, they chose the tent as their permanent abode. The snowblock dome of fictional fame was actually a hunting party's temporary shelter, seldom used for more than a couple of days. It was called an *iglusuugyk*, shortened to "igloo" in popular literature. The year-round home of these peoples was the skin tent, generally a low, rounded shelter of caribou skins supported by a network of thin wands. The design was perfect; any taller shelter would be blown away by the winds that scour the icefields; any other shape would require far too much heating fuel to be practical.

Early societies in forestlands never wanted for shelter. They had any number of basic tent designs, but most had some factors in common. They were formed of readily available poles bent into domes or tunnels, covered with skins or bark, and provided with vents for smoke exhaust. The utility of these rough shelters may be found in the record of the Massachusetts Colony. A 1674 journal entry records, "The best of their houses are covered very neatly, tight and warm, with the barks of trees, slipped from their bodies at those seasons when the sap is up, and made into great flakes, with pressure of weighty timbers, when they are green. The meaner sorts are covered with mats which they make of a kind of bull-rush, and are also indifferently tight and warm, but not so good as the former.''

The Pilgrim Gookin, writing in the same year, notes: ''Some [shelters] I have seen sixty or a hundred feet long and thirty feet broad. I have often lodged in their wigwams, and found them as warm as the best English houses.'' It might be noted that even English houses of the seventeenth century lacked proper insulation or central heating, both of which were present in the early Indian longhouses and wigwams!

MODERN TENTS

The early shelters were the product of several centuries of experimentation and adaption. Modern society has improved those designs with new fabric, breakdown aluminum poles, superb waterproofed and insulated components, and very light weight, but the best modern tents are nothing but further modifications of the ancient design. The essence of comfort and covenience lay in developing and adapting a design suitable for the environment in which it was used. That essential axiom is as true today as it was five centuries ago.

The modern trailshelter, with roots as deep as civilization itself, has become the model of efficiency. It provides extraordinary comfort and safety on the trail, and during times of extreme weather can be essential to the maintenance of life. The importance of a reliable portable shelter cannot be overstated; every survival manual includes shelter and water as the two most important physical elements in an emergency.

Most hikers and backpackers will fortunately never face threats to their survival on the trail. The vast majority will spend their recreational periods in relative safety, comfort, and enjoyment. The little backpack tent plays a major role in providing that creature comfort, protection from the elements, and aesthetic enjoyment of the outing.

Specialized Tents

The safety provided by the modern trail shelter is a factor of design. Although nearly all tents have the essential components required to protect the recreational hiker, not all tents can protect during extreme conditions. Some, therefore, have been further modified to cope with particulary difficult weather and terrain conditions. A typical lightweight backpack tent would be totally useless in the Himalayan highlands, *by design*. The extreme climate of the Himalayas requires a shelter that would be too heavy, too warm, and too expensive for the conditions that most of us meet. Fortunately, the outdoor outfitting industry has given us an enormous choice of designs, quality grades, and prices. The hiker, camper, or backpacker can easily select a shelter that will be adequate to his needs, yet not be an undue burden to his back or his pocketbook.

With few exceptions, the tent chosen by the hiker will provide wind and weather protection, have a floor to keep gear and people dry, provide sufficient space for activity (besides sleeping), and keep mosquitoes and other pests at bay. It will also furnish a degree of privacy, a genuine concern along today's more crowded trails. The modern tent does all of these, and is still light enough to carry with relative ease.

Waterproofing and Flies

The ideal backpack tent, to protect the hiker in

adverse weather, must have some provision for keeping water and wind from reaching the interior. This is usually accomplished in one of two ways; either the tent surfaces are water-resistant or a separate waterproof cover is included. Of these options, the latter is by far the most practical. The reason, simply enough, is that a canopy that will keep water *out* will also keep water *in*. A person generates an incredible amount of moisture as he breathes, and that water will condense on the inside of the waterproof tent. By morning, even in the nicest weather, the inside of the tent will be soaking wet. So, for that matter, will be the hiker, his gear, and everything else. It's a trifle discouraging to sit up in a sleeping bag, touch a clammy tent wall, and have a miniature rainstorm cascade down on everything inside. Unfortunately, that is often the scene in a waterproofed shelter.

To provide both comfort and protection, the material chosen for the sidewalls and canopy must be a fabric that breathes. Such a material, however, is also porous enough to let rain or snow through. The answer to the problem is a second roof, suspended slightly over the first, and completely resistant to water. Called a "fly," the second roof keeps the water away but provides air circulation over the inner tent, keeping everything warm, dry, and comfortable.

TENT NOMENCLATURE

To understand the differences in tent design, the reason those differences are incorporated, and the effect they produce, it will be helpful to apply some basic terms to parts of the tent. By discussing the purpose of each of the parts, it is relatively simple to see the effect a design change would have.

There are literally dozens of designs, but we've

illustrated the parts by drawing a composite tent. This configuration might not be found in a catalog, but there are several that are quite similar to our conglomerate tent. The components of the tent include the following:

CANOPY   The large, rectangular surfaces that form the roof. In some models this is coated with a waterproofing agent that negates the need for the fly but creates a serious condensation problem inside the tent. (*Note:* Some manufacturers are experimenting with new materials and absorbent surfaces that show great promise. Some of these developments are outlined in Chapter 2.)

RAIN FLY   The second roof that is suspended over the canopy of an uncoated tent. This allows adequate air circulation between fly and canopy, yet keeps all the water off the inner tent. It is probably the best arrangement yet devised.

SIDEWALL   Not present on all designs, but allows considerably more inside room with very little addition of weight. A few designs have quite high sidewalls and

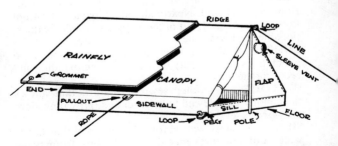

The actual design of a given tent may differ, but the parts will remain essentially the same. Knowing the proper names will help in discussing the differences in design.

are desirable for long-term camping or housing several people in one shelter. Many pyramid tents have exceptionally high sidewalls and are correspondingly heavier.

FLAP   The "doorway" of a tent. Some flaps are divided as illustrated, a few open only from one side or another, and some fold down from the top. A few models substitute a "tunnel" entryway and are especially good for heavy snow conditions. The flaps are usually equipped with an inner layer of mosquito netting. On warm nights only the nets need be closed, allowing comfortable breezes to blow through without the attendant insect problems.

END   Usually denotes the closed end of the tent, often equipped with a window or vent (also covered with netting) that allows cross-ventilation.

SLEEVE VENT   A variation of this is available on most tents, since any kind of heater will generate some carbon monoxide. Virtually all winter tents have such devices for allowing fresh air inside the tent.

FLOOR   Generally the floor is a waterproof component sewn into the tent. It keeps water and univited creepers out and helps insulate the occupants from radiated cold. Nearly all tents have a waterproof floor as an integral part of the design. It would be questionable to choose one without this feature.

LOOP   A device sewn in at support points, to which lines or pegs may be fastened for expanding and securing the tent.

PULLOUT   Another sewn-in feature that allows the canopy or sidewall to be extended, providing more interior space.

SILL   A short wall across the entrance that keeps water out and prevents dirt and debris from being brought into the tent when entering. The sill is particularly important in snake-infested areas.

POLE   One or more long supports that secure the tent in position. They are generally telescoping or sectioned aluminum tubes that can be shortened for easy transport.

PEG   One of several small sharpened devices that allow the tent to be secured against wind, seepage, or other hazards to comfort.

GROMMET   A circular device affixed to any part of the tent to which ropes or lines may be attached.

LINE   One or more long ropes that support the ridge of the tent.

ROPES   Side or end supports that allow the tent to be expanded for occupancy.

RIDGE   The top line of the tent; the point at which the canopy sections are joined. The similar point on the rainfly is not considered the ridgeline.

NARROWING DOWN THE CHOICE OF TENT

The beginning hiker will certainly be confused by the boggling array of tents and shelters in the outfitter's shop or catalog. At first glance, choosing the right shelter seems an impossible task, but in reality the various configurations are specifically suited to certain activities and conditions. The hiker must first determine his own interests and activities, and then find the tent that suits his needs.

No doubt a few people are going to fall in love with a particular tent and buy it, even though it might not be exactly what is needed. After all, individuality is a large part of outdoor recreation. If the object of his affection exceeds his requirements he will undoubtedly keep it, bearing the added weight or cost simply because he *likes* it—and the choice has been a good one. If, on the other hand, he has chosen a design that isn't quite up to his level of activity, a few chilly nights, soggy sleeping bags, or confrontations with curious little animals will convince him that a change is definitely in order.

The tent, by widest definition, is a portable shelter of skins, cloth, or canvas, supported by poles, usually fastened to the ground by pegs, and extended by ropes. That could range from a circus tent weighing several tons to a little backyard tarp to keep Fido out of the elements. Since we are concerned only with those tents used by recreationists, we can eliminate about 90 percent of all tents made from our considerations. More specifically, we'll want to concentrate on those that can be carried by self-propelled hikers and backpackers—about half the remaining designs. Wall tents, tent trailers, and other configurations for the vehicular camper will be discussed in chapter 6.

Disregarding the manufactured specialty tents, skin or other rustics, and the car-camper varieties, only a scant percentage remain for the hiker, backpacker, cyclist, or canoeist. Still, that means a couple of dozen basic designs from which to take a choice. It also means that there is at least one—and perhaps several—that will suit any particular activity. Choosing the proper tent from this list is not nearly as difficult as it may have appeared at first. It is simply a matter of understanding how each design applies to our chosen form of recreation, picking the individual model, and plunking down the ransom!

SITING THE TENT

Almost as important to safety and comfort on the trail is the question of siting the tent: i.e., what spot in all the wilderness is going to make the camper happiest. The site is usually considered more in terms of technique than equipment, but the two are so interdependent that they can hardly be separated. The proper site will have relatively level ground and a reasonably accessible source of water, be protected from wind and blowing rain, and keep the party safe from avalanche, rockslide, and flooding.

The site should also allow safe egress to sources of firewood (if a fire is permitted), the latrine, and other destinations that might have to be reached after dark. If the path runs alongside a swift stream or a sheer drop, the possibility of disaster is ever present. Proper siting will result in a safe, more efficient, and more comfortable camp than just randomly pitching in the first available spot.

In recent years another consideration has appeared that may overshadow some of the physical requirements—that of environmental awareness and our moral responsibility to the wilderness. With annually increasing numbers of hikers taking to the woods we must choose a site with certain considerations for our fellow hikers, lest the experience be diminished for everyone.

Before examining the factors that are physically appropriate for the camp, it is essential to consider the environmental and moral aspects of choosing the site. One of the primary responsibilities facing the modern camper is his impact on the land through which he travels. In many wilderness areas, deterioration of the more popular campsites and splendors has occurred through thoughtlessness, ignorance, and sheer numbers. Although many parks and forests now limit camping to designated areas to minimize the impact, large parts of the country still allow general overnight stops anywhere. It is up to each of us to preserve that special freedom by making a conscious effort to keep the land viable, clean, and desirable. The correct choice of campsite can do much to perpetuate the wilderness opportunity.

Foremost among the environmental considerations is our attitude toward the campfire, perhaps the most traditional feature of the trail camp. In many parts of the country—and especially the alpine regions—there is neither fuel nor reason for the evening fire. The development of lightweight backpack stoves has lessened the need for a fire in most places, and a horde of hacking and chopping imbeciles has removed nearly all the fuel, anyway. Moreover, the alpine wilderness is not a suitable place for a roaring bonfire.

In some forest and riverbank regions (and these are getting fewer each season) there is still a supply of waste wood sufficient for many warming and cooking fires. If the hiker is so fortunate as to find such a place, his fire must be kept as small as possible and fueled with waste wood that can be removed from the scene without essentially changing its character. The time of the unrestricted evening fire has long since passed; we should cherish those few times when one is possible as a special gift from a benevolent nature. More often than not, we'll get along with the stove and fuel we have carried along. The campfire, for all its charm, is not—and never has been—a *right* passed along to us by several generations of fur-clad forebears.

If a fire is possible and desired, it must be built on mineral soil cleared of all flammable debris and enclosed in a firepit. Afterward, it must be *completely* extinguished, the firepit erased from sight, and the stones returned to their original positions. No sign of the fire should remain and the camp should be left as natural as possible, ready for another group to enjoy on some distant day. If no safe firepit can be excavated, the fire must be given up. To subject the range and forest to the ravages of wildfire, simply for the convenience of the party, is the ultimate irresponsibility. Any person so selfish should be banished forever to the flame-resistant world of concrete and asphalt!

The hiker's responsibility to the wilderness extends far beyond the firepit and his own trash and wastes. The fragile meadow grasses, the dainty alpine flowers, even the hardier growth of the forests must not be sacrificed to comfort and convenience. In deciding on a site, the moraine or open sand is not nearly so inviting as the softness of the meadow, but there is simply no choice. The grasses cannot survive even a night or two of compression under the camp, but the open sand can endure a generation of sleepers with no visible sign—and it must be chosen!

The camp should be sited no less than 200 feet from the nearest source of water, both for environmental considerations and to avoid overnight flooding. Even though signs of hundreds of camps lie just along the shore of every lake and stream, we must choose a place that will neither pollute the water nor contribute to a quagmire. With restraint, the shoreline will someday recover, a source of joy to all who would visit there.

Thus, we will choose a site that will preserve and protect the wilderness instead of adding to the damage already there. With these environmental and moral attitudes firmly fixed in our minds we can get on about the nuts-and-bolts business of choosing the best possible place to site the tent.

The first requirement we noted was that of a relatively flat spot for the tent and the attendant activities of camping. The site should be free of overhangs, dead snags, or steep fields of loose rock or snow that might fall or slide into the camp.

Ideally, the campsite should be protected from

strong winds by a ridge or a stand of timber. It should be located on a shallow knoll, however, to provide good drainage and let evening breezes stir through. The knoll will allow rainwater to run off easily in case of overnight rain, and the breezes will keep the hordes of mosquitoes and other gnashers at bay. If the site is too well protected from breezes, the little beggars will swarm all night long. A few persistent types, of course, will buck a thirty-knot headwind to feast on succulent campers, but a breeze will help keep the number down a little.

The choice of campsite is really important to the comfort and safety of the party, but most often *all* the desirable elements won't be present. The mark of a good camper is how well he can adjust to those that aren't, making the camp a happy memory despite a rock under a shoulder-blade, the long trek to the spring for water, and sleeping with his head and feet decidedly downgrade from his middle!

There are many elements that contribute to the enjoyment of the outdoors, many of which are quite beyond the control of those who venture out. Some, like the weather, are subject to the whims of nature. Others—the route, equipment, and congenial comrades—can be determined by the hiker. Of all the equipment chosen, few items more directly contribute to the final success of the venture than the tent—that little shelter that becomes a home along the way. The tent eventually assumes the character of its inhabitant; it might be spartan and austere, or it might be equipped with the little amenities that indicate a desire for creature comfort. In either case, or anywhere between, the tent becomes an integral part of the wilderness experience. When it is pitched, it represents a tie with contemporary society; yet at the same time it is a living link with generations long past. When struck and folded in the pack, the tent is carried forward, ready to once again become an island of comfort in the back-country. Small wonder it occupies such an important niche in the inventory of equipment.

Satisfying both our spiritual and physical needs, the little tent is a relic from the depth of our collective history; it gives us the inspiration we need to survive in a complex social world. The same may be said of the whole wilderness adventure—and therein lies the charm of our moveable mansion!

CHAPTER 2

The Essence of Design

The modern designer has adapted many of the ancient
tent configurations to the needs of a legion of hikers
and backpackers. With newly developed fabrics and
construction techniques, the current models are just as
secure as the old styles, yet are considerably more efficient. They are generally very light in weight, surprisingly durable, and provide a degree of comfort un-
dreamed of by early nomads.

Just a few decades ago the average outdoor tent was
made of canvas, quite heavy by comparison with the
modern fabrics. The trail tent was yet to be devised; so
a rather large amount of canvas was lugged into the
woods (usually on horseback), a number of substantial
poles cut, and the base tent erected after hours of toil.
The whole affair was hardly what we would now
consider portable, but it was the best available.

By World War II the military had developed the
pup tent, a basic canvas shelter that housed two

people in the field. Although it was still so heavy that it required both campers to carry it, the pup tent was immediately seized by the hiking public as a godsend. It was cumbersome and inefficient by today's standards, but it represented the first real breakthrough in tent design. For several years the surplus supply of these shelters met the demand, and further development was forced to wait; the industry simply couldn't compete with the surplus prices.

Finally, the supply began to dwindle, the prices started up, and a growing gaggle of backpackers started looking for alternatives. The time was finally ripe for the development of a new breed of trail shelters, and the industry didn't take long to respond.

The hiker of today has a virtually endless choice of tents, each built to answer a specific need. Within the several design groups are a multitude of individual models, ranging from the sublime to the ridiculous in size, quality, weight, and cost. Even though the selection of a tent is too important to be dictated solely on the basis of price, we must look carefully at that facet; many tents are too expensive for most of us. Because of the diversity of design, however, there is a really serviceable shelter within the means of almost anyone.

In most cases a shelter will be chosen for the efficiency with which it meets its intended application. The summer soldier certainly doesn't need the protection (or expense) of a snowline expedition tent, but the technical mountaineer cannot trust his safety or success to the lightweight trail shelter. The demands of each outdoorsman are quite different, and a proper design is available to both.

On the following pages we will investigate the dozens of tents that represent the vast majority of backpack shelters, noting the uses, features, and disadvantages of each. Armed with this information, most hikers will have little trouble choosing the one that suits them best.

THE TARP SHELTER

Essentially nothing more than a flat sheet of protective material, the tarp might be fabricated of plastic, canvas, rough cloth, or coated nylon. The water-resistant nylon tarps are easily the best, but are priced accordingly.

There are many hikers who seldom use anything except a tarp. Among the many advantages, they cite a flexibility that is inherent to this design. It can, they argue, provide a certain level of shelter in almost any hiking situation. The tarp is unquestionably the lightest and least complex of the backpack shelters, but there are quite a number of disadvantages to it. The strongest supporters of this shelter are quick to defend it for aesthetic reasons. They claim it gives them a genuine sense of freedom, a greater communion with nature. That might well be, but it also

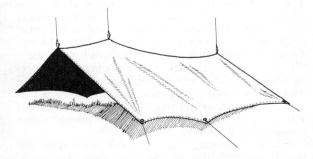

The simple tarp is quick, light, and easy—but it fails to provide the essential protection.

makes them especially vulnerable to soaking rain-
storms, whipping winds and dust, and the onslaught of
a squadron of starving mosquitoes!

The most serious drawback of the tarp shelter is its
lack of an integral floor. In almost every environment
visited by the recreational hiker from alpine ridge to
desert dune, the floor is a positive element of safety
and comfort. It keeps dampness from seeping up into
the sleeping bag, spiders and scorpions from setting up
housekeeping in a warm boot, and dirt and debris from
joining the party inside. True, a few dyed-in-the-nylon
tarpists carry a second sheet for a floor and some labo-
riously tie mosquito netting all around, but it seems as
though they are just building a modified tent of their
own. Nothing wrong with that.

From a positive point of view, the tarp is fun and an
interesting alternative to the enclosed tent that can be
used as a quickie shelter along the trail, or as a wide-
open shelter on a balmy summer outing. A lot of hikers
have logged some pretty pleasant outings with no more
substantial shelter, and when conditions are right, it is
a perfectly acceptable option. It would seem less than
prudent, however, to rely solely on a tarp to the exclu-
sion of an enclosed tent on the pack. A small plastic
tarp might sell for about $3, a good coated nylon style
as much as $30. Tarps weigh ridiculously little.

ONE-PERSON SHELTERS

The ultralight one-person shelters are among the
latest developments in tent design. They are not often
seen along most major trails of the country, owing not
to a defect in design or comfort so much as the fact
that hiking is not generally a singular activity. Most accepted guidebooks recommend at least two people
hike together for the obvious safety advantage. Any

number of hikers do set out alone, of course, and the one-person shelter is quite efficient for their needs.

Many of the more recent one-person designs use the backpack as an integrated component of the shelter. This tent actually amounts to little more than a good sleeping bag cover with a few accessories added. Construction is generally of a water-repellent fabric, sans rainfly.

The one-person tent almost always includes a sewn-in floor, mosquito netting inside the flap, and a basic venting system to reduce inside condensation. These devices seldom weigh more than a couple of pounds, yet are quite efficient for a wide range of conditions.

Because they aren't fitted with a separate rainfly, they are not particularly satisfactory under extremely wet conditions. Most one-person configurations are not recommended for alpine or deep winter use for two reasons: first, they simply don't provide adequate protection against the cold (though a fitted liner could help that), and, second, it is patently foolish to face the rigors of high alpine or deep winter camping without at

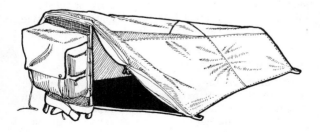

One of the newer one-person tents. It provides all the necessary protection, but prevents much social exchange along the trail.

least one companion. In those instances a larger tent would be the logical choice.

The one-person is constructed economically. It is really very small and will not accommodate two average-sized hikers. Putting two people in such a tent is like trying to sleep two in a single sleeping bag.

The one-person tent is at its best during solitary, midsummer hikes. It is quite a versatile shelter, and two people thus equipped might expand their hiking into practically every season of the year. For really difficult conditions a homemade liner (see chapter 4) should be incorporated for the extra safety and comfort it affords. It appears that none of the commerically available models includes a frost liner, even as an option. The manufacturers apparently agree that winter camping should be a more gregarious enterprise.

The one-person tents weigh from two to four pounds and reach the $60 bracket, although many are priced lower.

THE BACKPACK STANDARD TENT

This is probably the most widely-used tent in the world, the accepted favorite of the majority of all packers and hikers. There are many minor departures in design but it is essentially a two-person tent of un-coated nylon with an integrated waterproof floor, mosquito netting in the flaps and vents, and a rainfly. In a few cases the rainfly is an option, but it is a necessary expense. Because the canopy is uncoated, the rainfly must be added for comfort and protection.

Undoubtedly the best compromise between weight and features ever designed, the standard backpack tent will serve fully 90 percent of all hikers under every circumstance they might be forced to endure. It is light

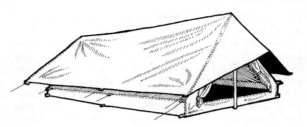

The most universal regular trail shelter, the backpack standard. Protection and comfort for two hikers in most circumstances.

and comfortable enough for all kinds of normal hiking, yet provides a remarkable degree of protection when a real storm blows up. We've kept our gear dry and wits intact as we waited out a two-day Cascade snowstorm in a flimsy-looking backpack tent, continuing the hike afterward with a minimum of fuss and bother. I've likewise endured an Olympic downpour in relative comfort while lesser equipped campers were scurrying for the nearest sauna. The backpack standard cannot be all things to all hikers, but it is the best all-round shelter one could expect to purchase.

There are some drawbacks to this elementary design, but they are more than overshadowed by the versatility it does have. For one thing, most models don't have a vestibule—a short compartment at the front for gear stowage, boot removal, cooking, and brushing off snow. That is generally a feature of specialized winter tents, but may be found in at least a few backpack models. The vestibule makes the tent a bit heavier and more expensive but quite a few dedicated hikers find it sufficiently useful to pay the price.

The backpack standard almost never includes a frost shield and most don't even offer it as an option. The addition of a shield or liner, however, extends the useful range of this design to virtually every seasonal variation one would expect to meet. It's well worth the investment of time and material to fashion one at home. The instructions for such a project will be found in chapter 4.

One or another of the many backpack models around will suit the needs of practically every hiker. Within the variations he will find the perfect shelter, depending on whims, pocketbook, and his own realm of interest. Those who journey to Katmandu will undoubtedly go equipped with a specialized shelter of great virtue, but even they will probably use a backpack standard for the bulk of their activity.

One of the great attractions of the backpack tent, beyond the obvious flexibility, is the straightforward design that contributes to its usefulness. It incorporates the most logical modifications of the simplest basic tent, allowing some further alteration by the inhabitant. Along almost any popular trail one might see some pretty imaginative features that have been added by the owner. Sometimes one of these seems like such a neat idea that we do the same to our own tent. Eventually a manufacturer will share our fascination with this little quirk and market a new model.

The backpack models weigh anywhere from 3 to 12 pounds and cost from about $20 to well over $150; yet they are just variations on the most successful theme in shelters. Just which end of the range is right for a particular person will depend on his own needs, whims, and ability to scrape up the change!

THE TUBE TENT

If the previous design is the best all-round shelter we can find, this type of tent has got to be the worst! It's

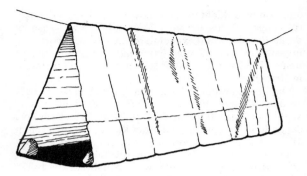

The tube tent, a dubious choice for the backpacker.

included here more as a bad example than a serious choice for the backpacker, but as long as we're at it we can give it a close look.

The tube tent is nearly always made of thin plastic, resembling an oversized garbage sack. In practice a line is run though the tube and suspended between two trees. The device is then expanded by placing a few heavy stones inside each corner. As if that doesn't sound silly enough, neither end can be closed, making the sleeper (if that's the proper image) easy prey for mosquitoes, gnats, wandering little animals, and an occasional hoot owl. If a breeze should stir to drive away the insects it somehow blows through the open-ended tube with a force all out of proportion to the outside velocity. It's a bit like sleeping in a wind tunnel. In the unlikely event that neither wind nor insect disturbs the camper, the condensation inside is roughly equivalent to a Burmese monsoon!

No doubt the tube tent is sufficient for the one-time-a-year hiker who chooses a perfect low-humidity weekend for the annual summer outing, but for anyone

beyond the bologna-sandwich-and-tennyrunner stage
it just isn't very practical. Perhaps I should be less
critical of this abomination, but our field tests of one
were among the worst nights I ever spent in the field.

Go ahead and try one if you must, but don't say you
weren't warned. These things usually weigh about the
same as a medium-sized decaying zucchini and cost
$3.88 or $2.99 or some such inane ad-agency price.

THE MODIFIED TUBE TENT

The modified tube actually has very little relationship to the configuration just discussed. It may have
evolved from the simple tube, but this modification is a
fairly substantial shelter that will serve many warm-
weather hikers. Called a "super tube" by some manufacturers, about the only similarity between this and
the instant tube is the open-ended design. The
modified tube usually has at least mosquito netting
over the openings. It doesn't have ends or solid flap

The modified tube is actually more of a backpack tent than a tube, suitable
for at least summer hiking.

panels, which can be something of a disadvantage in wet, windy conditions.

The modified tube is constructed of urethane-coated fabric, the wraparound floor being the same stuff in a heavier grade. The tendency of the material to accumulate condensation is partly negated by the open ends, allowing a bit faster evaporation. Still, on a humid night you might find a sizeable puddle under the sleeping bag.

The tent has aluminum poles fore and aft which allow a great deal more flexibility in pitching than an ordinary tube. From that point of view this tent is very similar to the more popular backpack standard, but the use of coated fabric and its open ends limit its usefulness for more active campers. Obviously, it cannot be fitted with a frost liner for winter, further limiting the conditions under which it can serve.

The general design of the modified tube includes peg-loops so boulders aren't needed to hold it in shape. A pullout on either side creates enough interior space for sleeping comfort.

The modified tube is relatively easy to pitch and has a reasonably decent configuration; so the future will probably see some genuine improvements in it. Without the end flaps and breathing fabric it is severely limited at present; a backpack or mountain tent is probably a better choice for all-around use. A great many hikers in moderate weather zones might find it a good bet, and for desert hiking or in the American Southwest it is a pretty comfortable shelter.

Because of the economy of material and construction labor a really good model can be purchased at a reasonable price. Most models weigh slightly over three pounds, including pegs, poles, and stuff bag. Costs generally run in the $50 bracket.

SNOW TENT

Although this tent has been specifically designed for snow-camping, it has been slightly modified for use in a wide variety of applications. It is not, by any means, an all-round design, but many hikers use it throughout the year.

Snow tents are distinguished by rather involved entrance and vent systems, a definite separated vestibule, and wide flaps along the bottom of the sidewalls. The flaps may be loaded with snow for added stability and warmth. Most models have a snow tunnel entrance at one end and a standard flap arrangement at the vestibule end. This allows occupants easy entrance, with cooking or other activity taking place at the vestibule exit. A few models lack the double entrance design, but those who do much snow-camping might be wise to avoid them. It is a trifle upsetting to have a lot of traffic through the evening stew, and outdoor cooking is practically impossible in heavy winter weather.

Since this tent is designed for winter operation—

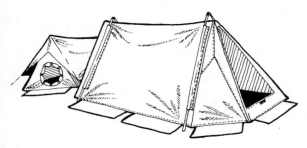

Only slightly less common on the trail than the standard lightweight, the snow tent is the most popular of the four-season shelters.

which means stoves and heaters are often used inside—the elaborate ventilation system is an absolute necessity. Every portable heating device, including a small candle, can generate massive amounts of carbon monoxide—a serious hazard to the winter camper. A constant supply of fresh air must be available any time a flame is burning, and the vent system must provide that supply. For the same cook-and-heat reasons the fabric of a snow tent must comply with CPAI-84, the industry standard of flammability for outdoor gear.

Campers in the northern states would be well advised to consider the snow tent for all their shelter needs. These tents are comparatively heavy and are usually quite expensive, but both factors must be weighed against the health and comfort of the party. The best arrangement is to have a good snow tent for winter and a lightweight tent for other seasons. Few of us can afford both; so it is better to be overprepared in summer than underequipped in winter.

In many cases the winter tent will require flukes or snow anchors instead of regular pegs. These may be found in any outfitter's catalog or may be fashioned at home.

Snow tents seldom weigh less than eight pounds; more often they weigh ten to twelve. The costs, with the fly and pitching accessories included, range from $150 to $200—and sometimes a bit more. They are generally of the finest materials and workmanship, incorporating the very latest in design and technique. Considering the inherent hazards of winter and high-elevation camping, the costs and weights of these complex shelters are fully justified.

LINELESS TENTS

Quite a number of self-supporting tents have appeared on the market during the past decade, and any number of hikers are receiving them with favor. The lack of outside guy lines reduces the amount of space required for pitching, a positive consideration along many of the crowded wilderness trails. In those areas where foot traffic has reached absurd proportions the design reduces the possibility of some numbskull kicking your shelter down in the middle of the night.

Most of the lineless tents are a modified-wall design fitted with tubular channels to support the canopy. The A-frame aluminum supports may be at the extreme ends or set partially inside the configuration as illustrated. The latter design produces a sloping end for expansion, allowing a lot of floor space but relatively less headroom. Those models with the supports at the ends of the canopy incorporate a vertical wall that allows much more inside living space.

The lineless tents usually include a good rainfly and can be quite easily fitted with a home-fashioned liner. The addition of these two accessories makes this tent a very good winter choice, although very substantial anchors are needed if high winds blow. The lineless fea-

Lineless, or self-supporting, tents come in a wide variety of grades and applications.

ture requires that all the stabilization be achieved by the pegs, or in winter by the anchors.

In many hiking situations the lineless tents are an extremely efficient shelter unit. They may be pitched on an area only slightly larger than their own floor space, require no nearby trees or bushes for guy line support, and are fully as comfortable as the backpack standard.

If there is any particular disadvantage to these designs it is the higher cost due to manufacturing and support material. Prices, however, are only slightly higher than for other tents of equal qualtiy. Lineless tents are somewhat heavier than similar-sized backpack standards, but again the difference is minimal. By and large, the lineless tents are an excellent choice for all-around camping.

Most models range from six to twelve pounds and may cost from $90 to $200, with about $110 being the median for a good quality unit.

THE OUTSIDE FRAME TENT

A popular variation on the lineless theme is the outside frame tent; a device that has an external aluminum support network that replaces ropes, pegs, and poles. They are similar to the "dome" tents that we will examine later, but keep the more conventional shape of the backpack tent.

As might be expected, the involved frame requires a bit of extra tubing, increasing the overall weight of the package. Outside frame tents are lineless, require no pegs or anchors, and can be erected on rocky moraines or deep snow with ease. The inside space is surprisingly large in relation to the apparent outer size.

Most outside frame tents are built of rip-stop nylon, have a substantial floor, and come with a contoured rainfly. As with most general-purpose tents, they have a netted window at the rear and a separate mosquito net inside the weather flap.

One disadvantage of outside frame models is the relative difficulty of stabilizing them in a high wind. Only a few have provisions for wind lines near the top, and all of them are difficult to stabilize with the rainfly installed. In areas of periodic, predictable rains they are quite comfortable, the overhang allowing the flaps to be left open in humid heat, yet protecting the inside from a soaking downpour.

Two-person models weigh about ten to twelve pounds, the four-person styles reaching as much as twenty-five pounds—completely out of the question for backpacking. The smaller units cost from $150 to $175 (sometimes much less) and the larger $200-$300 and sometimes more.

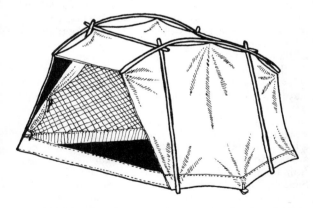

Outside frame tents vary from small to large, but many are too heavy for standard backpacking. They feature lots of interior space for their outside dimensions.

THE DOME TENT

From an engineering standpoint the dome is one of the most efficient shelter designs possible. The physics might be a bit involved, but let it suffice that the dome is exceptionally stable in wind, can bear great amounts of weight from snow or water accumulation, and provides the maximum usable interior space in relation to exterior size. The most popular of these tents can be pitched in a couple of minutes with a half-dozen fiberglass rods, and then moved to a more suitable site without disassembly should a giant boulder suddenly materialize under the sleeping bag.

The standard dome is made of nylon or dacron with a waterproof floor sewn in. The upper portion is a lightweight, breathing fabric; so a fitted rainfly is a necessary accessory. Most models include the fly as standard equipment.

The dome is essentially another lineless model but includes provisions for attaching a stabilizing network if a strong wind comes along. Deluxe variations include inside storage pockets, mesh side panels for cooling, and interior lines for hanging clothes, lamps, or other gear.

One of the early disadvantages of the dome tent was a special difficulty in striking. The long fiberglass support rods were joined by metal ferrules that sometimes resisted all attempts at separation. If the tent was weighted down by rain or condensation, the rods took a little extra bend and became almost impossible to get apart. More than one disgruntled hiker has returned from the trails dragging a sheaf of six-foot rods behind him, the fabric supports of his tent torn to shreds. The ferrules would become so stubborn that it became a choice of ripping the shelter down or leaving it permanently pitched in some forest glade. The manufacturers have nearly solved the problem, but it still occa-

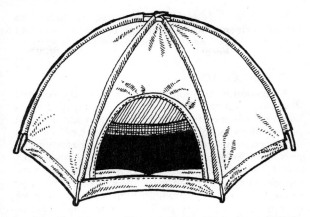

Dome tents have been around for a couple of decades, and are available in many sizes and models. Among the oldest architectural designs, they are comfortable and stable.

sionally rears its ugly head. By and large, the domes are an excellent form of shelter and most hikers have little trouble with them.

A modification of the dome that has only four supports over a rectangular floor is available. Actually, this configuration somewhat defeats the initial purpose of the dome, but is a very fine trail shelter anyway. One company calls its model a "wedge," which seems to describe it pretty well.

The rainfly for the dome tents is just a trifle heavy, but not enough to constitute a serious drawback. Considering the excellent protection from rain and cold offered by the fly, it is a pretty good investment in labor. Frost shields are not available—and fashioning one at home takes a certain amount of sewing wizardry—but a liner-equipped dome makes one of the best of winter shelters.

Various models weigh from under six pounds to nearly thirteen pounds, including fly, stuff sack, and supports. Costs range from about $100 to over $250.

THE TUNNEL TENT

A genuine innovation in trail shelters, the recently developed tunnel design has found many friends among the expedition/mountaineering fraternity. At present there is only one such tent on the market, but it has certainly lived up to the maker's expectations. It must have found its origins in the sheathed longhouses which the Pilgrim Gookin so richly praised, and the modern version is a fine piece of equipment. It is one of the most stable and comfortable shelters we have ever used, performing perfectly under the worst of conditions.

The tunnel tent is probably more shelter than most summer hikers would ever need and may even be a bit much for general camping, but when the wind blows or the snow starts drifting it is one of the very best places to put your faith—not to mention your gear, provisions, and tender body! The vaulted-arch design is vir-

A blend of ancient design and new materials, the tunnel is a recent shelter innovation that has been enthusiastically accepted by many mountaineers and foul-weather hikers. It is extremely stable and comfortable in the worst of storms.

tually unflappable (pardon the pun) even on a knife-ridge that would scare a snow leopard. The ingenious guy system keeps the tunnel rock-steady in a howling blizzard.

The design, despite its apparent size, weighs only a fraction over six pounds, including the optional vestibule and stuff sacks. It takes a little more effort to erect than some of the simpler tents, but it repays the labor many times over in safety and comfort.

The construction of the available model is every bit as good as the design. It consists of an inner shell of light ripstop nylon and an outer shell of water-resistant, urethane-coated nylon. The sewn-in floor is likewise waterproofed with urethane. The supports are of hollow fiberglass with aluminum ferrules, kept together by shock cords inserted through the centers. The design could conceivably lead to the sticking problem experienced in the older dome tents, but it has not been reported to be a problem with the tunnel designs.

The tent has been enthusiastically received by high-country hikers, but may take a little longer to be as well accepted by the occasional or flatland back-packer. Perhaps cost is a factor in that respect, but this tent could not be produced cheaply. Considering the excellent quality and exceptional comfort it provides, the tunnel just might be one of the best buys on the market. As previously noted, the final choice of a tent must be based on the requirements of the individual hiker, his activity level, and financial considerations. The dedicated hiker or mountaineer should give this tent some serious thought; it's among the best new shelters to come along in many a season.

The only currently available model weighs about six pounds and is priced just under $300, including the optional vestibule. A smaller modification of the tunnel is available at just under $200. It weighs about 3.5 pounds and might be just as good for the general backpacker.

EXPEDITION TENTS

The various expedition tents were developed to house long-term hiking and climbing parties under a wide range of weather conditions. Essentially a variation of the snow tent design, the expedition tents are constructed of the finest materials with the very best of workmanship. Many models include an optional snow liner and extralong fly that nearly reaches the ground. All include a cooking vestibule and intricate venting system, and almost all share the double-entry features of the snow tents.

The subject of some of the most intense fabric research in the industry, the expedition tents will soon be available in specially developed fabrics that are both breathing and waterproof. This seeming paradox is accomplished through the use of a microporous polymeric film of Teflon® to which fabric is bonded. Acting somewhat like an animal membrane, the film keeps liquid water out but allows vaporized water to pass through. The fabric merely protects the film from damage and abrasion. Such a tent really won't require a rainfly, but the manufacturers suggest carrying one along for the added wind and cold protection.

Some of the best models have a floor constructed of two layers of waterproof material between which a waffled insulating grid is placed. This produces tiny air pockets that help keep cold from reaching the party inside. This feature has been discontinued on some tents since new lightweight sleeping pads have been developed that are more efficient at insulating the sleeper inside.

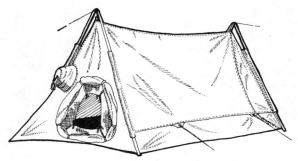

The best and most expensive of the standard shelter designs is the expedition tent, required for long-term camping at high altitudes and in bitter cold. Many have frost liners, cooking facilities inside, and special safety features.

The expedition tent was designed specifically for expeditionary use, but the design has proven highly adaptable. A few dedicated hikers carry one for all their general camping needs and have been fully satisfied with the performance. The expedition tent is not overly heavy, is quite comfortable in moderate temperatures, and is considerably better than a backpack standard for off-season use. About the only disadvantage is that is is too warm for many summer locales.

Nearly every outfitter carries an expedition or similar design of tent. For many this constitutes the bulk of their sales, it being so well adapted to a variety of conditions and uses. Weights range from about six to twelve pounds or more, including rainfly, and costs vary from around $125 to well over $250.

PYRAMID TENTS

The great majority of pyramid tent designs are more suited to car-camping and boat travel than to backpacking, but at least a few have been specifically designed for the hiker. Most pyramids, even of the backpack variety, are suited for three or four people. For the large party they are more efficient than a couple of two-person shelters, being slightly lighter than two of the latter. The use of modern fabrics has helped to reduce the mass that must be carried, but they are still quite a load.

The real beauty of a pyramid tent is the enormous floor area in proportion to the weight. Headroom is restricted along the sides, but the tent allows more efficient heating, plenty of sleeping room, and a good center for after-hike social activities. For the gregarious party with a deck of cards, the space is invaluable.

Some pyramid designs have been modified for expeditionary use on the theory that the larger space de-

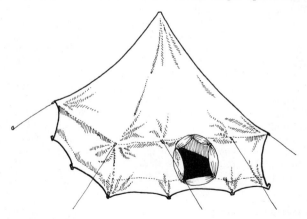

A popular design for vehicular campers, the pyramid tent has been modified for hiking and expedition work. It is roomy but relatively heavy.

mands and heating requirements can best be met with a pyramidal configuration. Equally important, the shape can take quite a load of snow without great loss of interior space. These tents have been on the scene of a great many major mountain ascents and have proven their designers quite correct.

Although acceptable for most outdoor activity, the larger pyramids aren't carried by most hikers simply because they don't need that much room. It just isn't particularly bright to carry a lot of extra weight if it isn't needed.

The drawbacks, other than size and limited head-room, are few: a centerpole that somewhat restricts the use of all that space, and a rainfly that is big and bulky. Otherwise the pyramid is a pretty darned efficient shelter—and a really comfortable choice for week-long stops at a base camp.

On the average a good pyramid-style backpack tent will weigh around 11 pounds with the rainfly and may cost from $100 to $175. The large, canvas models for car camps or river travel are covered in Chapter 6.

NET TENTS

A special family of tents has been developed for warm-weather activity and tropical camping. In these tents the solid canopies have been replaced by large panels of mosquito netting. Obviously, they provide protection only from insects or other such hazards and are of little defense against wind and cold.

The net tent must have a rainfly added for even minimal protection against the elements, and even then offers little warmth. It is excellent for the hot, dry desert conditions it was designed for. The tent is suited only to the reliably warm climates of the desert Southwest, the humid South, or the tropics.

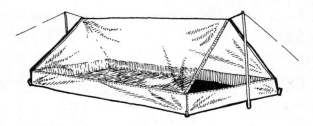

The net tents are suited to hot weather or high-and-dry camping only. They
are very light.

We've seen a few such devices pitched on midsummer Cascade and Rockies trails. They certainly give
the user a sense of open freedom not found in more
conventional shelters, but the threat of a sudden rainstorm or chill mountain wind would leave most
campers sleeping a bit uneasily.

One of the manufacturer's prime selling points is
"maximum breathability and a 'sleeping under the
stars' feeling." That might be well and good for a few
places, but the lack of privacy and protection restricts
this device to a very few North American settings.
What's more, the use of netting instead of a panel of
nylon reduces neither the weight nor the cost of such a
tent. This design should be considered more a novelty
than a serious choice unless *all* one's camping will be
done under hot or humid conditions.

Most models weigh about six pounds with the fly
and will cost around $50-$60.

PRICE, WEIGHT,
AND QUALITY CONSIDERATIONS

Once the basic design has been chosen, the field is
considerably narrowed. Yet a great many factors must

still be considered before the final purchase. Among these are the price, weight, and quality of the tent in question. A few general observations about these features can make any camper better prepared to make his decision.

The quality of the material is nearly always indicated by the price range, but that isn't a hard-and-fast rule. If two tents are of very similar appearance and size, but far apart in price, the more expensive is usually a higher-quality unit. Occasionally a manufacturer will try to make a few extra bucks because his tent *looks* like a popular model. A little close examination is required regardless of the price.

Fabric and Construction

The best of the uncoated tents is usually made of 1.9-ounce ripstop nylon. It is usually more durable, more costly, and offers more protection than an identical tent with 1.7-ounce material. Those figures indicate the raw weight of a square yard of the untreated fabric. You can quickly determine if the material is ripstop by looking closely at the weave. If every tenth or twentieth thread of the warp and woof (horizontal and vertical weave) is much thicker than those between, it is a rip-resistant fabric. Unless you've been around nylon for a long time, you'll have to rely on the manufacturer's label to determine the weight of the cloth.

If the fabric is waterproofed, you will find a dull, colorless coating on one side, usually the inner surface. If the tent is of a breathing fabric, the rainfly may be coated or constructed of a plasticized material. It is better to pick a tent with a coated nylon fly rather than one of the plastic rigs, which tend to deteriorate more easily. The same general guide applies to floor material; try to find a tent with a floor made of good-grade urethane-coated nylon instead of plastic. After a couple of years of exposure of heat, cold, water, and countless feet and knees, plastic has a habit of failing at the most inopportune moments.

Many states now require that all tent material be fire-retardant. That is a feature that adds weight to the finished product but provides an added degree of safety to those inside. A safety standard has been developed by the fabric industry that has generally been accepted by government agencies, although changes are being made in the standard quite regularly. Presently, the standard is known as CPAI-84. It denotes a chemical treatment the fabric receives. Many nylon and dacron fibers have a characteristic tendency to retard flame and are reasonably safe even if they aren't treated. A healthy application of common sense and reasonable care is an even better fire preventative in camp!

A good indicator of the quality of a tent is the manner in which it has been sewn. The best tents have a seam that has been folded and double-stitched, evenly, along both margins of the fold. Some of their cheaper counterparts are simply single-hemmed. Look at the seam carefully for signs of "puckering" or skipped stitches. Many of the better-quality units are sewn on a specialized machine featuring a "dual feed dog"—a device that feeds both top and bottom fabric layers evenly to the needle, allowing a smooth, unruffled seam to be produced. Many quality plants sear the raw edges of the nylon during cutting to prevent unraveling in the future. If the tent in question has a lot of raggedy edges and loose strands along each seam, it hasn't received this step and is likely to fail where a seared cut would not.

Very few manufacturers can seal their tents right

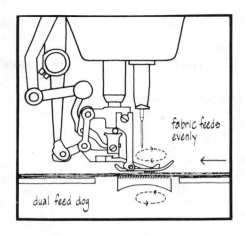

fabric feeds evenly

dual feed dog

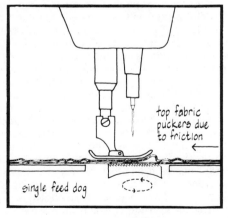

top fabric puckers due to friction

single feed dog

Better-quality tents are sewed on special machines (top) that almost eliminate the puckering sometimes caused by ordinary machines (bottom).

along the stitch. Each place that the needle penetrated the fabric may leak. None of those tiny holes can admit much water, but in the aggregate they can cause a leaking problem. After purchase it is wise to treat the seams with an elastic sealing compound, available at practically any outdoor shop. In most cases that step is probably not necessary, but if your activity includes much wet-weather camping it's pretty cheap insurance.

ACCESSORIES FOR SNOW-CAMPING

If a little snow-camping is on the agenda, it would be wise to choose a tent that can fairly easily be fitted with a home-fashioned frost liner. Instructions for this accessory may be found in Chapter 4, but the simpler the basic tent design, the easier it will be to make the liner. If the tent is to be pitched on snow, some kind of auxiliary stabilization will be needed. Standard pegs will not provide sufficient support in soft snow, but anchors will give the tent plenty of stability. You might choose to carry ready-made flukes or anchors, or just bury a stick tied to each tent line. In extreme wind conditions a little water poured over the anchor will cause it to freeze in place and provide a rock-steady support. Getting the line back the next day might be a bit of a problem, but at least the tent will still be there!

The basic elements of choosing a shelter, then, are the use to which it will be put, the quality and material needed to do the job, and the combination of weight and size that makes it comfortable for the user. Personal preferences, a touch of ego, and even the price must also be considered before a final choice is made. When all these are considered—and a few whims satisfied just for fun—the final selection shouldn't be too tough at all. When it has been added to the pack, slept in a few times, and carefully cleaned and dried after each outing, it will become as much a part of your outdoor enjoyment as the journey itself.

With a little attention and care, your tent will last for many years, providing a familiar place in the wilderness. Surrounded by the beauty of the land and filled with the joy and comradeship of the trail, it will become a living part of every adventure. Best of all, the trailside shelter encloses those special moments of recollection that cannot be diminished by time.

CHAPTER 3

The Alternative Shelter

The campsite, in one form or another, has long been a part of our literature and folklore. In the typical scene a rugged individualist is sitting around the dying campfire enjoying the final cup of coffee. As the last of twilight fades he tosses a blanket on the ground, pulls a corner of it around him, and sleeps. A nearby log becomes his pillow, a canopy of stars twinkles over him, and warm breezes accompany the sleep of the pure in spirit. The resting hero might be a cowboy, explorer, pioneer, or bandit. The background will change according to the story, but the manner of sleeping remains unchanged.

In reality, sleeping under the stars is a good bit more romantic than practical. Leaving aside the possibility of a drenching downpour, that scene would invariably have to include gnats and scorpions, a heavy dewfall, swarms of ravenous mosquitoes, and a bone-chilling breeze tugging at the bedroll. Completely overlooked in this fictionalized idyll is the sheer discomfort of the rocky ground, a log-stiffened neck, and a fitful night that left the vagabond feeling as though he'd been assaulted by a crazed buffalo.

The modern hiker and backpacker can follow in the painful footsteps of his mythical ancestor if he wishes, but chances are he'll endure the same uncomfortable reality if he tries. That present-day hiker who succumbs to that idealistic nonsense will, come morning, have to wring out everything but his pocket knife.

Certainly there are rare situations and conditions when a night under the stars is possible, and then it becomes one of the most pleasant experiences of the outdoors. More often, several factors will be present that make the unprotected night more of an ordeal than a pleasure. The same bugs, stones, and creeping chill that plagued the real-life old-timers are still around to bother the present generation of outdoors enthusiasts. So, before we begin our investigation of the alternatives to the trail shelter, let's understand that every party cannot, on demand, enjoy this free-form camp. The circumstances that permit such luxury are exceedingly rare. It is absolutely essential that every group in the wilderness carry an adequate, stable shelter on every trip. If the night is perfect, the tent may be left packed with the other gear, *but it must be available*! To head into the backcountry with the idea of "sleeping out," and no provision to do otherwise, is a foolish invitation to discomfort, danger, and worse.

BIVOUACKING AS A SPORT

Perhaps the simplest of all overnight stops is the bivouac, when the party just steps off the trail, snuggles into sleeping bags, and waits for morning. It might be the simplest, but it's also the least reliable way to get the needed rest for the next day's trek.

By definition, a bivouac is "an area in the field where troops rest or assemble, usually having no protection or shelter from enemy fire, or only tents, or shelter made from anything available." In our case, the "enemy fire" is nothing more than chilly winds and a multitude of biting insects, but that's enough. Nowadays, a bivouac is most often undertaken by technical rock climbers who must spend a night on the face of a mountain. They carry a short sleeping bag for this purpose, a device that covers only the lower body. The upper half is protected by a down parka, while gauntlets and a drawn hood complete the sleeping arrangement. Under extreme conditions the sleeper is physically lashed to the side of the mountain to prevent a slight shift or roll from being his last. It's a very uncomfortable situation that requires immense dedication to the achievement of the summit. The average backpacker would not put himself in such a position by choice; his bivouac is something quite different.

When the hiker is attempting very long distances in good weather, he might consider the bivouac as an alternative to the more formal camp, with the full knowledge that he will not rest quite as well. In this unusual circumstance the sleeping bag is spread on the open ground with a small tarp under or over it. If an evening shower or a heavy dew occurs, this scene usually becomes one of frantic scurrying and groping as the tent is somehow erected in the dark. The hiker and his gear are stuffed—along with a surprising amount of instantaneous mud—into the hastily pitched shelter for what remains of the night. The attempt to save time by bivouacking is often thwarted by such vagaries of weather and the inevitable clean-up the following morning. The fact that the hiker's boots were inadvertently left out in the rain only emphasizes the folly of his evening choice.

THE TARP SHELTER

Many hikers find that a semibivouac can be accomplished by pitching a very simple tarp shelter at the end of the day. In a few places the tarp can be erected in a matter of seconds, merely being tied to the handiest available tree and pegged down with a minimum of fuss. Actually, the shelter provided by the tarp is plenty for summer camping if rain is the only consideration. It will keep rain and dew away pretty well, but offers no relief from insects, chill, wind, or other discomforts. At this point, the camp is no longer a bivouac, but instead a rustic trail shelter.

The tarp is favored by many hikers as an alternative to the larger tent because it offers a fair degree of protection while maintaining a special communion with the wilderness. Unfortunately, that communion sometimes becomes a little more intimate than anyone wants, particularly is some small animal decides to investigate the camper and his gear. Most of us consider a glimpse of a porcupine, raccoon, or skunk as the highlight of the day—unless we become the unwilling object of its curiosity!

The tarp shelter offers practically no privacy, a serious disadvantage along many of the crowded trails today. Most of us realize that modesty will be compromised a little along the way, but we don't care to be exhibitionists, either. A number of recent guidebooks have suggested some quite elaborate arrangements in which the tarp is enclosed at either end with windbreaks and sight-screens, fashioned from a couple more smaller tarps. Undoubtedly that will work, but it seems a darned sight easier just to put up the tent and be done with it.

There are many places that do lend themselves to the use of the open tarp, and one may be rigged for the night in many ways. A tarp might be set between whatever supports are at hand, or the tent poles may be used to erect it in the open. The shape the tarp will take will depend on the conditions at hand and the cleverness of the camper. The tarp offers an un-challenged feeling of freedom to the tent camper, but the disadvantages must be considered before the tent is left unrolled on the pack. As already noted, it's a real nuisance to pitch the tent in a driving downpour.

Along the trail we are apt to find almost every conceivable form of tarp, ranging from big canvas affairs to flimsy plastic dropcloths that are purchased in the neighborhood five-and-dime. A few years ago there appeared on the market a new tarp that featured a nylon sheet to which was bonded a metallic membrane for heat reflection and waterproofing. Known as a "space blanket," it is a fairly substantial cover in an emergency, can be used as a tarp by the single hiker, and reflects available heat readily. A larger size can be fashioned into a decent shelter for two, but in common with other tarps it offers no protection against insects or cold weather.

The best tarps available at present are exceptionally fine nylon affairs with a dependable bonded water-proofing agent, well-constructed grommets at the margins, and three or four support tabs sewn into the ridgeline. These can be pitched in a number of ways to provide reasonably good shelter. A few dedicated tarpists fit their units with large triangles of mosquito netting and a separate ground cloth (another tarp) that effectively convert it into a basic backpack tent. Thus rigged, it makes a secure and mighty comfortable

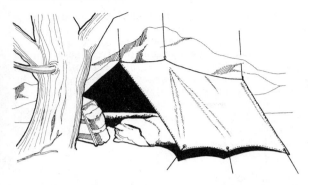

When bivouacking, the simple tarp can provide a pleasant, comfortable camp—if rain, chill winds, and the creepie-crawlies stay away!

shelter, but in reality it's little less than a complete mountain tent. It seems wiser to start with a tent in the first place.

FINDING SHELTER ALONG THE WAY

Some fledgling hikers decide to set off along the trail with the idea of finding adequate shelter along the way. One can never be sure just what opportunity might present itself (or what lack might be found), but the result is almost always a disappointment. Experienced hikers have learned to rely on their own tent instead of the doubtful availability of something rustic.

Public Trail Shelters

Not so many years ago it was possible to find substantial shelters built along the more popular hiking routes, but that is no longer the case. The majority of the forest shelters have fallen victim to vandalism, attrition through age, or dislocation of the trail. If you are fortunate enough to find a good trail shelter on the way, it will likely already be filled with other hikers. There is a growing movement, particularly in the western forests, to restore or rebuild the old shelters, but it isn't gaining much favor among park and forest officials. The chronic plagues of underfunding, overcrowding, and vandalism make the outlook a little bleak.

Natural Shelters

The party may sometimes, through happy coincidence, end their day's journey at some place where a natural shelter exists. It might be a rock overhang, a shallow cave, or even the large root wad of a windblown tree. A rooflike stone overhang is a good shelter in most cases, though such spots are characteristically damp in the temperate forests. Deep caves are rather rare in most parts of the country, and shallow ones should be investigated thoroughly before a camp is made. Those with solid rock walls and ceiling should be sound enough to occupy, but in most instances will already have at least one native resident. The cave is no less appealing to a colony of mice or a bobcat than to a hiking party. The former might make the night a little more than interesting for the lug-soled claim jumpers!

The rock overhang can be greatly improved by adding a makeshift windbreak or extended canopy. Either can quickly be rigged with a small tarp and a few yards of light line.

A root wad might be chosen for shelter, but this primitive cover is not without certain hazards. In most

cases the wad creates a depression in the ground that will collect water at the slightest rain. More often, the trunk side of the roots will be the safer shelter, but a small tarp will usually be needed to provide the required degree of protection.

If windy or stormy weather is anticipated, the root wad is an exceptionally poor choice. At least a few instances have been recorded where another windfall has broken the original downed tree, allowing the trunk to be pulled upright by the sheer weight of the root mass. At that point, the roots swung back into place, crushing anything that might be under them. Such an incident is rare, but not without precedent.

A downed log that is suspended by a knoll or another log may be used for shelter whenever one is found. The problem with that arrangement—as with most primitive shelters—is that it is least effective when it is most needed. Quite often, the resultant structure is over a depression where rainwater can collect, making the hasty camp a quagmire. In good weather, of course, such a shelter is sufficient.

Trail Huts

Along some of the eastern U.S. trails we are starting to see a system of overgrown "huts" that provide lodging, meals, and an altogether-too-communal atmosphere. In theory, we applaud the efforts of the Appalachian Mountain Club and other groups who have provided the huts in an effort to reduce the impact of too many people on too little country. Despite the nobility of the endeavor, I should prefer to give up hiking entirely than to spend my nights in a place of someone else's choosing, eat food provided by someone else, and pay as much for that privilege as I might at a good motel. Perhaps the reestablishment of the old trail shelters would provide a good alternative on those trails, but that seems an unlikely prospect. As long as freedom and enjoyment are paramount, there will ever be those of us who will carry our own shelter and provisions. For us, anything less would diminish the experience to such an extent we would simply give up and go home.

Those "catch-as-catch-can" hikers who hunt for natural shelters are definitely in the minority, since there just aren't enough overhangs and caves to go around. We will talk in chapter 7 about building shelter from living trees, but that is strictly an emergency measure. In that respect, we must realize that even the cutting of small poles for tarp supports or boughs for beds is an irresponsible and unlawful act. Our moral commitment to the wilderness dictates that we take everything we will need into the forest—and bring back everything we have carried in.

SHELTERS MADE FROM SNOW

The winter hiker, despite his need for a more reliable, substantial shelter, has a great many more options than his summer counterpart. In winter there are an almost unlimited number of opportunities for tentless camping, owing to the very nature of the winter environment. The cold and snow that create the greatest need for shelter also provide one of the best materials for building it.

The off-season hiker, with a little effort and knowledge, can produce some very comfortable shelters of snow. In a few cases it is only necessary to burrow into a well-packed snowbank, shape and compact the living area, and set up campkeeping. On large flats or treeless terrain, the compacted snow may be cut into large building blocks for the constructing of a more elaborate overnight home.

If the simple burrow is chosen, the location must be in a low drift or face rather than in a tall, avalanche-prone slope. The shelter location must be selected to minimize any danger to the party.

The natural depression that is formed about the trunk of a large tree is an acceptable spot for constructing a burrow shelter, since there is little possibility of a slide or drift closing the entrance during the night. In nearly any snow shelter there will be a need for auxiliary air sources, since the compacted snow is remarkably air-tight. The proper construction of these air passages will insure a sufficient flow of fresh air even if drifts or a heavy snowfall occur.

The simplest of the constructed snowblock shelters is a trench over which large blocks are set in an ''A-frame" configuration. Before cutting the blocks, it is necessary to tromp the snow down firmly and allow it to "set" for about thirty minutes. This results in a compacted material that will not easily fall apart when erected. The compacting process produces some moisture within the snow mass, and the thirty-minute wait allows it to refreeze into a very stable surface. The blocks should be removed from the trench area to reduce the amount of cutting and digging required.

The igloo shelter is a great deal more difficult than the trench shelter, requiring the spiraling blocks of snow to be locked in place by the top, "keystone" block. Once completed, the outside of the igloo should be smoothed as much as possible and any melt that might occur used to freeze an ice "skin" on the dome. A certain amount of melt will occur inside from the heat generated by the occupants; so at least some provision must be made for carrying water away from the sleeping area. In most cases, a short sleeping "bench" is constructed inside. The sleeping bag must be insulated from the snow by a small tarp or foam sleeping pad.

The simple snowblock "A" trench provides at least minimal shelter.

The various snow shelters require some strenuous building activity with certain tools that make the job easier. The winter hiker intent on providing an alternative shelter should carry the items necessary, including a light snow shovel and a snow saw or machete.

The winter shelter can be a comfortable and efficient alternative to the tent, but as in the summer situation the camper should never be without an adequate portable shelter. The tent is just as important— perhaps more so—in the winter environment as it is in summer. A quick thaw or even a lack of snow will leave the underequipped in a desperate fix.

Alternative shelters consist only of bivouac techniques, simple tarps, roofed structures along a few trails, and the handful of natural shelters outlined here. In every case we must carry our shelter with us using these unusual temporary houses only as an interesting departure from the ordinary. To begin a journey into the backcountry with the hope of finding shelter at random is nothing more than an exercise in discomfort, hardship, and outright danger.

CHAPTER 4

Making Your Own
Portable Shelter

The backpacker has always been something of a do-it-
yourselfer, fabricating many items of his inventory at
home. In the early days his preoccupation with home
equipment construction was largely a matter of necessity; more recently it has been in the interest of
enhancing the outdoors experience.

The pre-boom hiker was forced by the unavailability
of many items of gear to make his own, from the basic
backpack to climbing hardware. After the industry
evolved into today's giant complex there was little
need to spend long hours over the sewing machine or
workbench. Industry was supplying everything one
could need, often at a cost lower than hand-fashioned
items. Still, there were those who took pride in their
ability to make a pack or gimmick better than they
could purchase. At least a few of those self-motivated
individuals are still around, building some extraordinary outdoor equipment that suits their individual

needs. Against the competition of today's highly pres-
tigious manufacturers of outdoors gear, it's pretty
satisfying to make a custom bit of equipment for yourself.

The home-fashioned shelter is not one of the easiest
projects for the do-it-yourself craftsperson, but it can
be one of the most rewarding. A clever designer-
handcrafter can put together a special tent of the very
highest quality material that incorporates all the features he would like and possesses a comfort almost impossible with the factory unit. At the same time he will
get the deep personal satisfaction that comes from
making it himself, at perhaps only half the cost of a
comparable manufactured unit.

The would-be tentmaker should first decide what
design will best suit his particular range of hiking
endeavors. The most popular choice among this determined group of home craftsmen is the standard
backpack tent, since it is easily the most flexible of
designs. Fitted with a rainfly and frost liner, it can
satisfy practically every tenting need. The fact that it is
easier to construct than most of the other models
doesn't hurt a thing, either!

MATERIAL

The question of materials is probably the most difficult for the neophyte, since tent fabrics are not com-
monly used in any other project. Depending on the
style and complexity of the proposed tent, the budding
tentmaker will use from four to ten different types,
weights, and shapes of material before the thing is
done. It is important that we understand the applications—and limitations—of each of the fabrics that will
be included.

Some of the materials conventionally used for tents

include nylon taffeta, nylon pima cloth, silicone-treated nylon, and Egyptian cotton. There are other materials on the market, of course, but the majority of tents are made from these. (Egyptian cotton is just the generic name for the weave and grade of a particular fabric. It normally comes from Alabama, Texas, Florida, or just about anywhere else cotton is grown.)

Most modern hikers use nylon in construction of their shelter. It's true that some forms of cotton pack-cloth are still used by a few traditionalists, but recent research has proven the value of nylon for general pack, tent, and outdoor use. Those who wish to use the heavier cotton duck or pack-cloth materials will have little trouble finding it (even in fire-resistant or water-repellent grades) but they will have to contend with greater weight, the tendency to mildew, and considerably greater maintenance effort than with nylon.

Nylon has a few disadvantages when compared to other fabrics, particularly in inability of the fiber to absorb any moisture. Condensation of water vapor can occur on the surface of even an uncoated style, causing drops to form rather quickly and drip on the occupants of the tent. The more porous lightweights, however, allow most of the vapor to pass through before the problem occurs. The advantages of light weight, elasticity, toughness, and ready availability more than make up for the problems; so a good nylon fabric will make up the body of our tent.

Tent Body

The canopy, sidewalls, end, and flaps of a tent make up the body, generally constructed of a single type and weight of material. The most popular choice for this purpose is uncoated nylon in 1.9-ounce weight. The weight figure, incidentally, refers to the actual measured weight of one square yard of fabric. It is relatively simple to determine the quantity of material needed for the tent and thus figure the weight of each component. In most cases it will be quite light theoretically; the addition of poles, pegs, lines, and the carrying sack will bring it up to the actual on-the-back finished total.

There are several waterproof coatings that may be applied to nylon, and many tent floors and rainflies are constructed of such treated fabric. For reasons already discussed in Chapter 1, however, the project ahead will be of an uncoated, breathing fabric.

The fabric chosen for the body of the tent will be a ripstop weave, in which every tenth or twentieth thread is considerably heavier than those in between. The larger-diameter threads impart greater stress-resistance to the fabric, making it more difficult to tear than a single-weight layer. Ripstop is only microscopically heavier than a plain weave, but it can bear heavier use and strain without damage.

Floor and Rainfly

The floor and rainfly of the tent must necessarily be waterproof to keep hiker and gear from getting wet and cold during inclement weather. The floor will also have to withstand considerable abrasion, weight, and the pressure of objects inside. Elastic coated fabrics will do well for the fly, but the floor will almost have to be a plasticized form of nylon. There are several such materials available at yardage shops and outdoors supply stores; just be sure to choose one heavy enough to take the punishment. The best of these are Fiberthin® or Coverlite®, the former coated with vinyl and the latter with a neoprene compound, or similar fabrics. The floor material should be a five-ounce fabric because of the heavy wear it will experience, but the fly may be constructed of a lighter stuff. There is at least one polyurethane-treated nylon around that weighs just 2.6 ounces and makes a dandy fly. A little heavier material won't hurt, since the average rainfly contains only about seven yards of material.

Whether the rainfly is the same stuff as the floor or a lighter grade doesn't matter so long as both are well treated with a synthetic, elastic waterproofing agent.

The New Miracle Fabric

We talked earlier about the need for using a breathing fabric for the body of the tent and a waterproof one for the fly because condensation would leave the whole inside of the tent resembling a shallow puddle. As one might expect, some scientist has come along and upset the old apple-cart with a newly developed fabric that does both the necessary jobs. It might sound a little paradoxical, but there *is* a material now available that allows water vapor to pass through quite readily, but is almost impervious to liquid water. A tent of this material will let breath and other vapors *out,* but won't let rain and snow *in.* To campers, who have suffered the indignities of the weather for centuries, this new stuff may sound quite impossible, but it works.

Presently there is only one manufacturer producing this miracle fiber, but there will likely be others before very long. At the time of this writing, the only such material available goes under the advertised name Gore-Tex®, and it is truly a remarkable substance. The theory behind the material is a little involved, but is essentially based on the size of the pores in a coating at the built-in electron charge of the substance. In practice, the tiny pores are large enough to permit the passage of tiny vapor droplets, but not large enough to allow drops to get through. Additionally, the larger drops assume a negative electrical charge that is effectively repelled by a similar charge on the coating. What the hell; we aren't here for a treatise on chemistry. Let's just accept the fact that such a remarkable fabric exists and we'll all be using it for something in the wilderness before many more years go by!

Loops, Pullouts, and Accessories

The points at which the tent is staked down, the lines attached, and the poles set will all be made of nylon webbing. This material is available in various weights and widths. The peg and rope loops might be just half-inch stuff on some tents, but the points at which the poles are inserted are usually about an inch wide to accommodate a small grommet. In the project ahead we will be using one-inch webbing for both; it simplifies shopping and construction. Strap-grade webbing is used on most tents (including ours) since it is sewn and reinforced as it is manufactured. Unfinished webbing just isn't strong enough for the strain points.

Tapes are used in reinforcing strain points on many tents, particularly things called pullouts and ridge loops. The several outside-frame tents we have already discussed use plenty of tape for reinforcement, but the simple backpack tent we will make requires none of it. Instead, some large triangles of heavier nylon are used as a support for the line loops and grommets.

Cotton tapes are used for finishing the rough edges of mosquito netting and might be employed on the edges of the flaps or other raw cuts. The tape chosen for this project should be a finished variety that has both edges woven. It won't require folding or stitching to prevent the edges from fraying.

Best Thread to Use

Nylon thread is superior for sewing the tent because it has the elasticity to match the fabric. It is difficult to use, however, requiring some experience and the lightest possible tension adjustment of the sewing machine. Those who lack experience should consider dacron threads. Dacron doesn't stretch, but that can be a mixed blessing. The thread may cause the more elastic material to pucker during construction. With a little care in aligning the edges to be sewn, dacron shouldn't present much of a problem.

Cotton thread is of no use whatsoever in making a nylon tent. It will mildew, eventually rot, and the whole shelter will collapse around your ears some night! A few seasons ago we saw a tent to which the floor had been attached with cotton thread. That was an unusual practice, even for the low-cost imports—and this was one of them. The young hikers using it were appalled when they tried to roll it up and the whole floor fell away. The dealer was equally dismayed and replaced the unit with a considerably better model and his apologies. As is true of most reputable outfitters in similar instances, the firm has since removed that particular import from its inventory.

The materials for a decent mountain tent consist of those outlined above, or others of equal quality. They have proven themselves over the past few years to be strong, reliable, and relatively inexpensive. The tent that the enterprising outdoors person will make from the following instructions will be likewise constructed.

If a sleeve vent were to be incorporated into the design, it would be made of the same body material. So, for that matter, would a vestibule, storage compartment, or a second story.

Ties

Among the accessory parts of the tent are the ties, little strips of cotton tape that are used for joining the flaps, keeping the rear window cover in place, or fastening the rolled flaps back for airing the tent. Cotton is chosen for this task since it tends to stay tied a lot better than nylon. The same slipperiness that makes nylon shed dirt and water also makes it a regular bear to try to keep tied.

Netting

One of the prime protective tasks of the trailside shelter is that of keeping hungry mosquitoes and other insects away from the tender body of the hiker. This is accomplished through the use of mosquito netting. The chosen fabric should be one especially designed for that purpose. There are many open-mesh fabrics around, but only one with a "leno" weave is suitable for mosquito nets. In this weave, sometimes known as a "marquisette," the warp strands are twisted around each filling yarn to keep them from pulling apart or opening. The mosquito netting should be of nylon for the same reasons that material is chosen for the solid panels. It will be necessary to finish all the edges of the netting with a good cotton tape. Construction details are outlined at the appropriate points in this chapter.

SEWING

It is entirely possible to make a tent without a sewing machine. After all, several thousand generations did it long before the device was invented. Still, few of us have either the skill or the patience to complete a modern nylon tent by hand. Most machines have a wide variety of stitches that can be quite valuable to the home tentmaker, but only a simple basic stitch is actually required. What *is* needed in making a tent is the knowledge of how to make several different kinds of seams and hems. Each has a specific purpose in the making of outdoor gear, and it's pretty hard to substitute something else for the proper material connection. None of the seams that we will use are particularly difficult, but you might practice a bit on some scrap material before you jump feetfirst into the project.

This book is not intended to be a basic course in sewing, but it is possible to learn a little about the essentials before putting your tent together. All of the sewing can be done on the simplest of machines (even a fine old treadle!) with a standard needle. A strong dacron thread is highly recommended for the actual construction of the tent. Even though nylon is better for matching the stretch of the fabric, it is almost impossible for the average home sewer to use. The tension adjustment for nylon is so critical (and difficult to accomplish on noncommercial machines) that dacron is by far the more practical alternative. The slight puckering that might be caused by dacron will have little effect on the appearance or usability of the tent.

Plain Seam

In this seam the edges to be joined are merely laid together and stitched about ¼ inch in from the edge. A

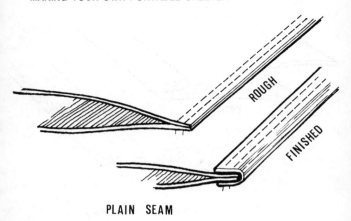

PLAIN SEAM

The plain seam may be "finished" with fabric tape before stitching.

second stitch is set about ⅛ inch below the first to provide added strength and prevent raveling. The stitch is used to some extent in the tent proper, but is more widely used for the frost liner and other rough accessories. The plain seam is "finished" by adding a binding tape along the joined edges before the seam is sewed. This seam is rather weak for canopy or floor construction, but is excellent on edges that suffer little stress.

Hem Seam

This is similar to the plain seam, but the edges are folded before stitching. They are either folded one time for a rough hem or twice for a finished hem, as illustrated. The finished hem seam is excellent for edg-

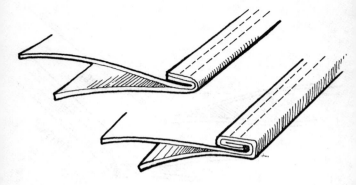

The hem seam is finished by tucking back before sewing.

ing one layer of cloth, such as would be done along the edge of a rainfly or the edge of a flap. When the finished seam is double-sewn it becomes many times stronger than the raw fabric.

Flat-Felled Seam

This is a common method of joining the large pieces that form the canopies or floor of a tent. In the event the fabric isn't large enough to cut the canopies or floor from a single piece, the flat-felled seam is used to join two separate pieces that will be large enough. The seam can be finished as illustrated, but is usually only made rough, especially when joining nonwaterproof materials. If the joint in question will be subjected to quite a bit of stress, as would be the case in a floor or rainfly, the finished seam is chosen for its extra strength.

Top-Stitched Seam

This seam is seldom used in tentmaking, but it might prove handy if you are going to design storage pockets or provide a separate vestibule in your tent. The top-stitched seam is quite valuable for outside-frame tents; it is the method by which the tubular frame channels are attached to the upper side of the canopy. As illustrated, the top stitch may be either rough or finished, the latter being much the stronger.

Insertion Seam

In most sewing projects this seam is used to join a single piece of material to two adjoining layers. In tent-making, however, it has been modified to join the floor

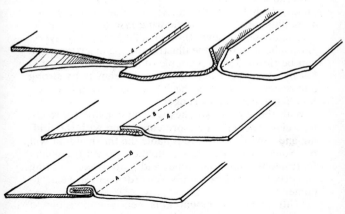

The flat-felled seam starts like a plain seam but may be turned sideways to complete or rolled to make a finished seam.

The top-stitched seam is seldom used in tents, except to add storage pockets or vents. It may be rolled to finish before sewing.

material to the sidewalls and upper tent. For such purposes, the lighter body material is folded into sort of a Y as illustrated, and the flooring inserted into the Y. The seam is then sewn through all the resulting layers. As can be seen from the illustration, the insertion seam can be finished with a couple of added folds, but it is hardly ever necessary. The rough seam is as strong and water-repellent as the fabric; so it would be useless to make it much stronger.

With these basic stitches we can construct a really first-class shelter. The more care taken with the folding and sewing, the more reliable the finished tent will be. Some of us are pretty impatient to get the whole thing done, but the time and care taken during construction will be amply rewarded in the years to come.

With home equipment it is nearly impossible to produce a *perfectly* straight hem down the side of a canopy, but the craftsman will make it as neat and straight as possible. Each change of direction in the line will give rainwater a tiny niche in which to collect as it slides down the side; so it is just a matter of "the straighter the better" when it comes to comfort and dry pajamas.

There will be a few special sewing techniques used on isolated parts of the tent, but those will be covered as that particular facet of construction is discussed. They mostly involve such things as drawhems, closures, and getting zippers that will zip in place. They are neither complicated nor difficult; we can cross those hem-stitches as we come to them.

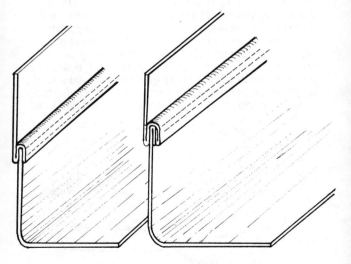

The insertion seam has been modified to join the floor and sidewall of a shelter. It provides a juncture that is almost waterproof.

MAKING THE BASIC BACKPACK TENT

The do-it-yourselfer who tackles a project as involved as a shelter, even as simple and small as the one described here, must be prepared to spend a few hours and experience more than a little frustration on the task. Chances are he'll finish with as good a tent as he could buy, at just a fraction of the retail cost. Equally important, he will come to have a better knowledge of his gear—and himself—and will better appreciate the whole wilderness experience because of it.

The design we've chosen is as straightforward and simple as can be imagined (see Fig. 1); yet it will serve most backpacking requirements quite well. The main purpose of this whole project is to demonstrate *how* a tent is made; modifications in design, adding features according to your own desires, and variations in sewing or construction techniques are not only possible, but are encouraged! Once the process of building a tent is understood, it's really quite easy to add a vent, lengthen the sidewalls, or even make the whole thing wider or longer. With just a little imagination and some

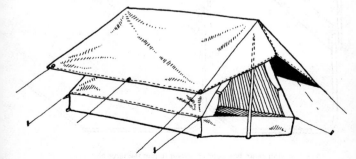

Fig. 1. The tent project with rainfly.

quick math you can significantly change the design to suit yourself.

The level ridge was chosen for ease of sewing. It might just as well have been one of the lighter sloping-ridge models or even something else. We could have included a catenary cut along the ridge to reduce a few wrinkles along the sides, but it just didn't seem worth it. A catenary cut, incidentally, is the ridgeline cut on the same curve as would be produced by a chain hanging freely from the end points and allowed to touch the lowest point of the desired curve. Big deal! The mathematical curve was theorized by some high-falutin' Greek who probably never even *tried* to sew his own tent! Anyway, our experiments showed that even without the catenary curve this tent can be pitched just about as smooth and wrinkle-free as any other.

For ease of demonstration (not to mention cutting and sewing) the design includes vertical end and flaps. It is a little roomier to provide at least a sloping rear end, but it really isn't worth the trouble for the amateur tentmaker. If you really want to, you can convert the design into a sloping-end model with only a little extra effort.

The material for the tent will include 1.9-ounce ripstop nylon for the canopy, end, and flaps. The floor will be a vinyl-coated nylon of about five-ounce weight, and the rainfly can be the same material or a somewhat lighter grade. The line and peg loops will be of a strong nylon webbing, while the few ties for the window and flaps may be a very light, finished cotton. The window and flaps will have the added protection of mosquito netting finished with one-inch cotton tape. The entire tent will be sewn with a good, heavy-duty dacron thread. The machine will be fitted with an ordinary needle, even though the insertion seam that

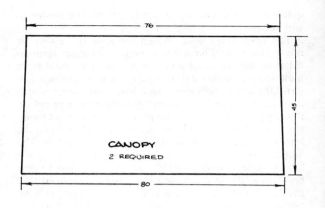

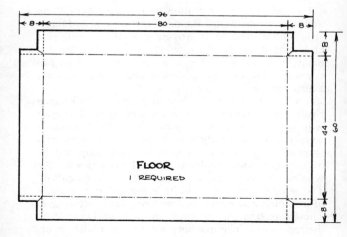

Fig. 2. Dimensions of the backpack tent.

joins the upper tent and the floor will be sewn through several thicknesses of material. The nylon is so light that even the multilayered seam only amounts to the equivalent of a couple of layers of heavy cloth.

If the tent is to be made exactly as it is drawn in Figure 2, you will need the following materials.

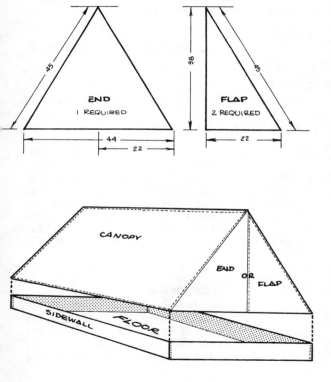

UPPER TENT

    6 yards of 1.9-oz. ripstop nylon (48 inches wide)

    1 yard of heavy nylon pack-cloth for reinforcement (48 inches wide)

    1½ yards mosquito netting (48 inches wide)

    7½ yards of 1-inch cotton tape

    1 yard of ½-inch cotton tape

    2 yards of 1-inch nylon webbing

    3 zippers and 2 grommets (see text)

FLOOR

    2.75 yards of 5-oz. vinyl-coated ripstop nylon (60 inches wide)

RAINFLY

    6½ yards 3- to 5-oz. vinyl-coated nylon (36–40 inches wide)

    10 grommets

These are the essential materials for the tent itself; you'll need ropes, lines, pegs, and poles for actually pitching the finished product in the field. It is quite possible to make your own poles and pegs, but it might be just as simple to get them from a nearby outfitter or order them from one of the many outdoor catalogs around. You might have to get one a bit longer than you need, but a few minutes with a hacksaw will bring it down to size.

Cutting Out the Upper Pieces

    The nylon should be spread on the floor and the pieces carefully marked before any cutting takes place. Many people will find it easier to transfer the pattern to a piece of newspaper first, and it seems a pretty good idea. The dimensions shown in Figure 2

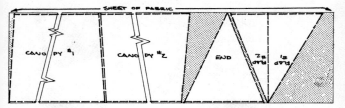

Fig. 3. Proper layout of parts on the raw material will avoid wasting fabric.

are finished size. *Be sure to allow ½-inch margins all around for hemming and assembling the tent.*

As you can see, the patterns for the end and flaps are simple triangles. The pieces can be cut according to the illustrated layout (Fig. 3) to conserve material.

Please note that there is a window in the rear of the tent. Most people find it easier to complete the window, covering flap, and mosquito netting before assembling the upper canopy. The front flaps and netting zippers, however, are best left until *after* the rest of the canopy has been completed. As you will see, it is about impossible to install the zippers properly until the canopy is done and joined to the floor section.

Assembling the Canopy

I found the following method the easiest way to assemble the tent. You may wish to deviate from this procedure in your own work, and there should be no difficulty in getting it all together if you go your own way.

Cut out the twelve-inch-square window hole in the center of the rear piece. Following the illustrations, bind the netting with one-inch cotton tape. Sew the

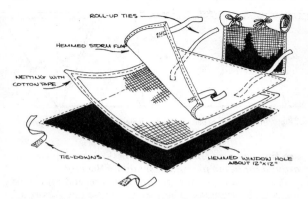

ROLL-UP TIES

HEMMED STORM FLAP

NETTING WITH
COTTON TAPE

TIE-DOWNS

HEMMED WINDOW HOLE
ABOUT 12"×12"

Fig. 4. Detail of end window. Sew netting all around, flap and roll-up ties
only along top of window.

netting in place with a finished plain seam as shown in
Figure 4. The hemmed flap (with the ties already attached) is sewn in place. The end is completed by just
sewing the roll-up ties and the closing ties in place.

Assemble the upper canopy by sewing the ridgelines
together using a flat-felled seam. A finished style is
best, but a rough flat-felled seam will work just about
as well. The seam should be completed with at least
three sewn lines, since the ridge is called upon to support most of the strain put on the tent. The seam
should be on the top (outside) of the tent.

Sew the finished rear end panel to the canopy, one
side at a time. The side and end panels are pinned
together (pins about every six inches) to prevent slip-
page as the actual sewing takes place. The unfinished
hem seam can be used for this operation, although a

finished hem seam looks nicer and will probably add a little to the finished strength of the shelter.

Pin flaps that will close the tent—and their corresponding mosquito netting flaps—in place and sew them to the canopy panels in one operation. That is, sew both the netting and the solid flap at one time to the proper part of the canopy. The netting should be edged with one-inch cotton tape all around before the actual sewing is done. The zippers that finish and close the front entrance will actually be installed on the netting flaps (rather than the solid flaps) for ease of construction and use. The solid panels will just be tied with cotton ties to keep the wind and cold out.

The hem seam is again employed at this stage of construction. The finished hem seam is to be preferred, but a rough hem seam will work. With the completion of this step, the upper canopy portion of the tent is essentially complete. All that remains is to attach it to the yet-unmade floor and put the zippers in place.

The upper portion of the tent, however, will be subjected to a great amount of physical strain when it has been pitched. The lines attached to the front and rear will be fairly tight and at sharp angles to the ridge. The light canopy panels, when subjected to even a moderate breeze, will be strained all out of proportion to their fragile weight. It's necessary, therefore, to add some reinforcement where it will do the most good—at the actual points of stress.

Before the upper section is added to the floor, it will be necessary to put two triangular reinforcements at either end. These panels (see Fig. 5) will be cut and fitted individually, sewn inside the ridge ends, and the loops sewn *outside* the reinforced section. Cut the panels from the heavy pack-cloth about a foot long, according to the finished shape of the canopy. Sew them in place on the inside of the tent; then add the loop of

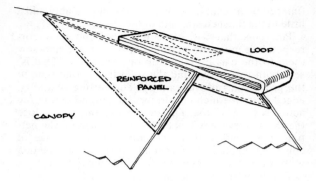

Fig. 5. Canopy reinforcement.

nylon webbing. If a grommet is to be inserted in each loop to accept a tent pole—and it is strongly recommended—the loops should extend about six inches past the end of the tent. When the reinforcements are installed and the loops are sewn on, the canopy can be laid aside until the floor is complete.

The Floor

Cut the floor section out according to the plan, making sure to allow one inch of hem material at each corner as shown in Figure 6. The four corners will be folded and sewn to roughly form a "box" that will measure 44 by 80 inches. The corners are made by folding the one-inch tabs up (step 1), folding up the sidewalls to match the tabs together (step 2), and sewing the tabs to complete the corner (step 3). Before sewing these points, insert two loops of webbing in each corner. These loops will be needed to peg down

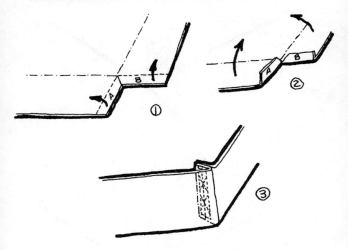

Fig. 6. Forming the corners of the "tub" floor.

the tent and to extend the sidewalls. The loops (Figure 7) are placed at the top and bottom of each corner joint and should extend about 3 inches outside the corner. When the loops are inserted, sew tabs "A" and "B" together with a rough, plain seam (see Fig. 6). The corners should be sewn no less than three or four times to provide the added strength that will be needed in the field. Since our floor is designed to include the sidewalls and doesn't require cross-hemming (unless the material at hand was too short or we made a mistake in cutting), the completion of the four corners with their loops constitutes the entire construction procedure. The floor is now ready to be fitted with the partially completed canopy.

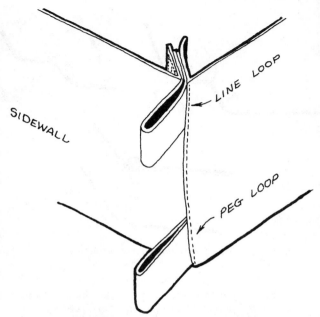

SIDEWALL

LINE LOOP

PEG LOOP

Fig. 7. Installing peg and rope loops at sidewall corner before sewing.

Fitting the Floor and Canopy Together

Fitting the floor and canopy together is the most difficult stage of construction of the entire tent; yet it is
not as tough as it might look. The secret to this is to pin
the canopy and floor together all around, carefully
from the insertion seam across the back, and repin it in
place. I recommend that you form a rough insertion
seam (rather than a finished seam) in two sewing
stages as shown in Figure 8. In making the insertion

seam, do the rear first, completing both sewing steps. This gives you the solid base from which the side seams can be finished. Once completed, the insertion seam provides a virtually waterproof and rip-resistant joint between the upper section and the heavier floor. Note that the front wall is quite untouched and the center and bottom portions of the flaps are likewise unsewn. They will be finished as the next step in construction.

Finishing the Flaps and Front Sidewall

Finish the flaps and front sidewall by adding the three zippers. The vertical zipper will join and finish the center line of the mosquito net flaps, while the two bottom zippers will finish and join the net flaps and sidewalls. Make sure the zippers *close* in the direction shown in Figure 9 or you'll find yourself a prisoner in

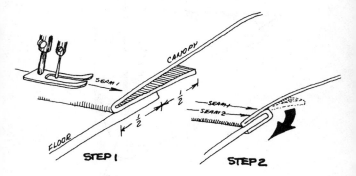

Fig. 8. The insertion seam is best sewn in two steps. The second seam may be double-stitched for added strength.

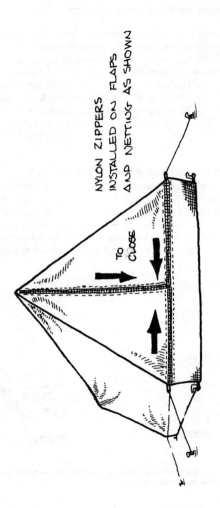

NYLON ZIPPERS
INSTALLED ON FLAPS
AND NETTING AS SHOWN

TO
CLOSE

Fig. 9.

your own creation! The zippers usually come with sewing instructions, but are very simple to put in, as shown in Figure 10.

Installing the Ties

The tent is now essentially complete except for adding the light cotton ties that will be used to keep the flaps closed during inclement weather and out of the way when things are nice. The ties are installed at the center line of the flaps and along the canopy edges as illustrated in Figure 11. The basic tent is now complete, with only the rainfly needed before setting out afield.

MAKING THE RAINFLY

No matter what the weather looks like, however, you had best not dash headlong from the sewing ma-

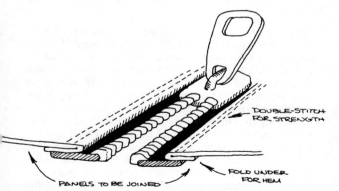

Fig. 10. The zippers should be double-stitched for integral strength. Nylon-coil zippers are best for tents and other outdoor gear.

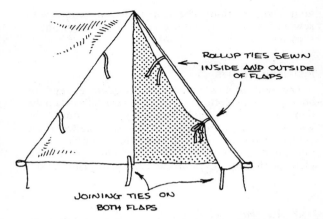

ROLLUP TIES SEWN
INSIDE AND OUTSIDE
OF FLAPS

JOINING TIES ON
BOTH FLAPS

Fig. 11. Ties of one-inch cotton are used to keep the rolled flaps out of the way or to tie them closed in inclement weather. The ties should be about six inches long for ease in tying.

chine before the rainfly is done. Leaving the changeable weather aside, the fly might be needed if the canopy is somehow damaged on the trip. It can be pressed into service as an emergency shelter, make a nice sun shield or windbreak for a rest stop, and serve as a simple shelter on especially nice evenings, if the dratted bugs don't make a nuisance of themselves.

As long as we are on the subject (and just about to start making one) we should talk a bit about the importance of the rainfly. Its usefulness in rotten weather is obvious, but the value of the fly is sometimes underestimated when things are warm and summery.

The few inches of space between the fly and the canopy provide very important air flows during extremely hot periods. Any number of summer and desert campers have suffered heat prostration while inside their tent because of a temperature some twenty or thirty degrees higher than the outside air. The lack of cooling breezes and the tendency of the tent's color to attract heat may drive the inside temperature into the hundreds, dangerously affecting those inside. The addition of a fly in extremely hot weather can reduce the inside temperature as much as fifty degrees, providing considerable comfort along with a margin of safety. The fly isn't terribly hard to make—and it is an absolutely essential part of the tent.

The fly for our tent is just as simple and straightforward as the basic tent itself. We've chosen to design one that provides a good overlap at either end to keep blowing rain from soaking the tent, yet requires a bare minimum of cutting and sewing.

To keep it all as easy as possible, we use grommets instead of loops to suspend the fly. The canopy angle is much shallower than that of the tent, allowing plenty of free air space between the two surfaces. Since the same poles are used to support each structure there will be contact right at the ridgeline, but it is a minimal amount. The greater area of the uncoated canopy is well separated from the fly, allowing easy escape of water vapor that would be trapped if the two surfaces were in total contact.

The steps required to make the fly are few and simple. First, from the coated nylon material, cut the two panels as shown in the accompanying diagram. Be sure to leave the one-inch hem margins at each end as indicated.

Join the ridgelines (point A to point B *only;* see illustration of rainfly pattern), using a flat-felled seam. It should be a finished seam, but may be left rough if too much difficulty is encountered in sewing it. If a lighter (three-ounce) material is chosen, the finished seam

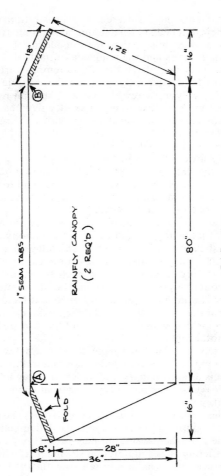

Rainfly pattern.

should be accomplished with very little trouble. Using about an inch of each panel for seams will leave a thirty-six-inch canopy on each side. At the smaller angle produced at the ends of the fly, this will easily protect the tent from rain and blowing snow.

Using the one-inch tabs at each end, join the end panels as shown, using a rough plain seam, sewn three or four times for strength. The fly should then be edged with a basic, unfinished hem. Make sure that the hem is applied on the underside of the canopy where no rainwater can collect.

Insert ten grommets as shown for suspension. When the fly is installed over the erected tent, you will need about six to eight feet of light nylon line in each grommet. Don't make the mistake of trying to tie these lines

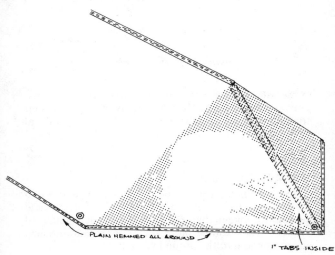

PLAIN HEMMED ALL AROUND

1" TABS INSIDE

Rainfly end detail.

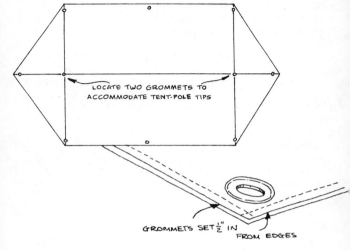

LOCATE TWO GROMMETS TO ACCOMMODATE TENT-POLE TIPS

GROMMETS SET ½" IN FROM EDGES

Placement of grommets in rainfly.

to the same tent pegs that are supporting the sidewalls. The result will be a badly drooping fly, almost constant contact with the uncoated tent, and a very wet and bedraggled band of campers inside!

THE ACCESSORIES

To erect the tent it will be necessary to secure two breakdown poles and a dozen pegs. The poles should be slightly longer than the thirty-eight-inch height of the tent. They will be more secure if they are pushed an inch or so into the ground when pitching. The poles can be made of aluminum tubing, or you may prefer to order ready-mades from the catalog. You'll likely have to buy two forty-eight-inchers, but a minute or two with a hacksaw will take care of that. The pegs need only be about six inches long and might be of aluminum or plastic, or even little sticks of wood.

The finished, erected tent and fly is shown in Figure 1. It is actually quite a stable and comfortable shelter, even though it would be a bit crowded for more than two average-size campers. It is not really suited to group activities, but it might accommodate three *very* congenial friends in a pinch.

About the only thing left is a stuff bag large enough to pack the tent and fly. Stuff bag is really something of a misnomer; carrying bag would certainly be a more proper description. The carry bag can be made of the very lightest waterproof nylon, but don't settle for less than that. An uncoated carry bag may leave the tent wet and miserable even before you get it up! The bag,

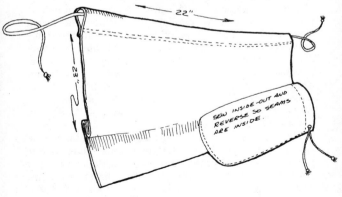

22"

23"

SEW INSIDE-OUT AND REVERSE SO SEAMS ARE INSIDE.

Simple carry bag.

made from material measuring twenty-three by twenty-two inches, will be about twenty-three by ten inches when finished and will carry the tent, fly, pegs, and poles in one neat little bundle. The accompanying illustration pretty well tells the whole story. After all, you just finished making a whole darned tent; a carrying bag should be child's play!

WINTERIZING THE BACKPACK TENT

If a lot of winter camping is on the agenda, it will be more comfortable—if not downright necessary—to make a frost shield for the backpack tent. The shield provides a much warmer surface on the inside of the tent as well as an insulating layer of air between it and the outer canopy.

The best shield is made from a washable fabric such as flannel or rough cotton. The winter requirements of camping dictate a lot more hours inside the shelter than in summer, and the shield will get soiled quickly. Flannel is inexpensive, warm, and porous enough to prevent any serious condensation inside the living area. Unfortunately, flannel and similar fabrics aren't even remotely flame-resistant; so one must be especially careful of the auxiliary heating and lighting devices that are very much a part of winter camping. There are some recently developed applications that will improve the flame resistance of flannel and other common fabrics; so it might be good to look at them before selecting a material.

The frost shield is nothing more than a smaller version of the original tent, designed to fit inside it after pitching. Obviously, the liner will be installed at home before the trip, but it still amounts to an almost complete inner tent. The liner includes a floor, sidewalls,

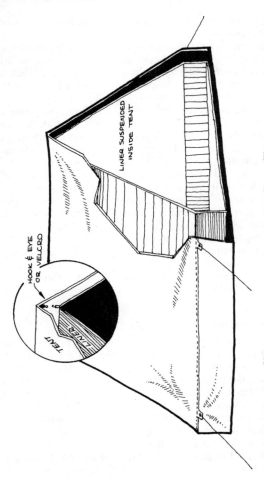

The frost shield, of heavy cotton cloth, is suspended by hook-and-eye, Velcro®, or some other attachment about two inches inside the canopy of the tent.

canopy, and end, but it doesn't need added zippers or other closures.

The frost shield may be hung from the inside of the tent with a hook-and-eye arrangement, suspended from the outer shell by nothing more elaborate than a few simple ties, or attached to the outer shell with Velcro®. The choice is up to you and your ambition.

To give the exact dimensions of a shield would be a trifle difficult, since not everyone will be making one specifically for the backpack tent covered earlier. In most cases the shield will be constructed for a tent already in the builder's possession. The dimensions, therefore, will almost exactly parallel those of the basic tent with enough size reduction to allow about two inches of air space between the structures. The best method of designing a homemade shield is to pitch the tent as cleanly and tautly as possible, take the inside measurements carefully, and then transfer the design to paper. After the measurements are made, reduce every dimension by *one inch*. After hemming, that will provide just about the desired air insulation between the layers.

Directions for Making a Frost Shield

Assuming here that a shield will be built for the backpack tent we have just made, let's look at the step-by-step procedure for making the liner.

Draw the pattern required on a large piece of paper. After the drawing is done and you can visualize the shield you will make, go back inside the tent and check the measurements against those on the drawing. Once satisfied that the drawing is accurate, transfer the layout to the chosen fabric.

Cut out the pieces and sew them as you would the tent. The entire frost shield will be sewn with unfinished plain seams, all on the *outside* of the shield, the reverse of the technique used on the basic tent.

Sew the appropriate fasteners on the outside of the shield (see illustration of frost shield) and attach the corresponding fasteners to the inside of the tent. Make sure the hangers are at least two inches long, so the shield will hang loosely inside the stretched tent. If the hangers are too short, the liner will touch the inside of the canopy, reducing the insulating advantage it is designed to provide.

A good frost shield can be designed for virtually any kind of tent you might be using. The winter liner will be a lot more difficult for a tunnel or dome design, of course, but will be relatively easy for almost any other kind of tent. The comfort provided by the shield is well worth almost any effort you make to produce it, and backpackers being the kind of people they are, it seems fairly easy to get someone to help you over the rough spots.

I've spent many winter nights along the trail in a tent without a liner, and other nights in tents fitted with well-made do-it-yourself shields that fit reasonably well. Given the choice, I'll take the liner every time.

The instructions we've given for making your own shelter and accessories have been necessarily complicated at times, but they should be reasonably easy for anyone to complete. It is important to take a little time and care when cutting and sewing. The cost of fabric is enough that you won't want to produce an unusable, slipshod shelter, and there is absolutely no point in wasting material that costs both time and energy to produce. If you are one of those who really enjoys a home project but you don't feel that fabric is your medium, find someone who can help you with the techniques. As an intelligent alternative, you might enroll in a short course on basic needlework and sewing.

Such courses are available at most community colleges, adult education centers, and even several of the country's leading outfitters. As a last resort you might look in the local library for a beginner's book on sewing or contact a yardage store in your town where some form of group education is available. It really isn't as difficult as it might seem at first, and the satisfaction you can gain from living afield in a shelter of your own creation is immense.

There is every reason to believe that you can produce a fine shelter at home for much less cost than a factory model of equivalent quality. By the same token, you can modify a design you've seen elsewhere into a tent that precisely fits your unique needs—and simply isn't available from the standard outlets. In any case, the construction of your own outdoor equipment can be a significant phase of enjoying the total wilderness experience.

In the final accounting, the outdoor experience is incredibly complex. It is adventure, learning, the appreciation of nature's magnificence, and a better understanding of ourselves. As we improve our skills, learn to be more self-sufficient, and gain a deeper enjoyment of the world about us, the experience grows into something quite unmatched in any other pursuit.

Just as our pleasure in the outdoors is enhanced by the rare opportunity to watch a peaceful animal family at play or to see an especially lovely sunset, so is it improved by the realization that we are secure in a shelter we have made with our own hands.

A night spent protected from outside storms in a shelter we have made ourselves is the extra little reward for an extra little effort—and it's fun!

CHAPTER 5

Interior Decor

The point has already been emphatically made that the tent is one of the prime factors in the safety and comfort of the camping party, but there are other considerations that make a big difference, too. These are the accessories, as it were, to the basic shelter. Obviously, the tent is there to keep the party out of the wind and the rain, but by itself it makes only the most spartan of life-styles possible.

The next most important factor in comfort (and in safety during extreme weather conditions) is the sleeping gear provided for each hiker. The best of shelters is not quite enough if the sleeping bag isn't warm enough to allow the proper rest between hiking days. We assume that the backpacker has chosen the rest of his equipment on the basis of his own need, and therefore has an adequate sleeping bag. The accessories, then, are those gimmicks and devices that improve the living and sleeping arrangements inside the shelter.

Some individuals consider an austere, demanding life-style quite necessary to their camping trips. In many cases, these are people who live a rather luxurious life at home, and they seem to need more than just a change of environment for their total recreation. I confess to being quite different in that respect; I vastly prefer a more-or-less comfortable situation whether at home or in camp. Each hiker will ultimately evolve his own routine and his own degree of comfort along the trail—and that's what the whole thing is about!

At almost any popular campsite you can find setups that rival the best lakeside resorts—and others that are quite fitting for Attila the Hun. In most cases, the inhabitants of each type of camp have chosen to live in the manner they do; this chapter was written for those who want luxury but don't know how to achieve it.

SLEEPING COMFORT

Next to having a stable and secure shelter against rain, wind, insects, and things that go bump in the night, a comfortable sleeping arrangement is most important to the average backpacker. He will depend on his sleeping bag or bedroll for this.

The Sleeping Bag

It is interesting that our collective outlook on the basic sleeping bag has changed. It wasn't so many years ago that a controversy raged among the outdoor fraternity over the relative merits of the bag as compared to the old-fashioned bedroll. Back in 1916 the two leading camping writers of the day engaged in a long-running argument that practically assumed the dimensions of a feud concerning the sleeping bag.

Horace Kephart, author of the two-volume *Camping and Woodcraft* series, equated the sleeping bag to a rubber boot, claiming that anyone who indulged in such an unsound mode of sleeping would surely be prone to catching cold immediately upon arising. Dr. Edward Breck, in *The Way of the Woods,* chastised Kephart for not giving the sleeping bag a fair trial. His bag (called, in those days, a "sleeping pocket") was "easier to use than camp blankets, did not get kicked to pieces quite as quickly, and could be evacuated in the event of fire just as readily as could open blankets." I don't doubt it!

The modern hiker and backpacker has the advantage of nearly six decades of sleeping bag development, and the camper afield with two army blankets and a down comforter is about as scarce as hen's teeth. The down- or dacron-filled sleeping bag has become perhaps the most consistent feature of the trail camp.

Most campers today desire to sleep as warmly and comfortably as possible without becoming overheated or unduly confined. The invention of the box-foot or barrel sleeping bag has done a lot to alleviate the old cramped feelings of the campers, and a medium-weight bag allows the sleeper plenty of warmth without being overcozy. Many bags have zippers that can be partially opened at the foot or head end to regulate the heat inside. To sum up, they are pretty darned comfortable, and far surpass any other kind of field sleeping arrangement.

When the weather is cold, there are several techniques that improve sleeping comfort. First, of course, is to put the bag inside a good field shelter. The temperature inside a nylon tent is about ten degrees warmer than the open air outside. That varies with the weather, but removing the bag from the wind will

make at least that much difference. Keeping the bag
dry makes an even greater difference, since the combination of wind and dampness produces a high wind-
chill factor.

Sleeping Pads and Mattresses

Insulating the bag from the ground not only im-
proves the comfort of the sleeper by the padding effect, it significantly increases the temperature inside
the bag. For example, a closed cell sleeping pad
between the bag and frozen ground can raise the
temperature inside the bag by at least another ten
degrees. There are many kinds of sleeping pads and
mattresses around, and most of them are nice in cold
weather. It might be wise to look at the various sleeping pads and mattresses from the standpoint of both
physical comfort and insulation.

Quite popular for summer hiking, the average air
mattress is either a plastic or neoprene device consist-
ing of several interconnected air tubes. The mattress
supports the sleeper on three or four inches of
confined air, providing a very comfortable platform
that keeps sticks, twigs, and the omnipresent rocks
away from tender shoulder-blades and hips. The air
mattress, however, tends to get cold and stiff when the
temperature drops. It has no insulating ability and may
even cause the sleeper to be colder than if he were on
the tent floor. Air mattresses really aren't recommended except for the summer campout in Aunt
Maud's backyard!

As for folding cots, backpackers aren't particularly
concerned with these abominations. They are usually remembered with some bitterness from Lake
Ochobokee summer camp or "Army days." A few vehicular campers will drag one along in the summer,

and they seem to work fine on those heavy-gear-and-hot-summer outings. They are reasonably comfortable, but they also provide no insulating value to the sleeper. About the best thing that can be said for the camp cot is that it gives you a place to store things out of the way. It's pretty hard to slide an ice chest under the sleeping bag for the night, but the backpacker probably won't have an ice chest, either!

Foam pads, a relatively recent development in the backpack arsenal, are lightweight, comfortable insulators that can make a significant difference in the quality of a night's sleep. They are available in either open-cell or closed-cell models, and are generally only large enough to cover the neck-to-thigh area of the sleeper. There really isn't much reason to make them longer, since the legs tend to stay warmer than the torso during the night, and the legs don't dissipate quite as much internal heat.

The closed-cell pad provides slightly less compression comfort than the open-cell variety, but the closed cell is a better insulator and doesn't absorb as much moisture when wet. Either pad is ridiculously light and easy to carry, the average pad weighing about six to twelve ounces.

A slight refinement on the bare pad, a covered sleeping pad is usually an open-cell pad with a removable, washable cover. The advantage of the washable cover is obvious; however, there is almost no difference between the bare pad and the covered pad in either their compression or insulation value.

One of the neatest sleeping devices to come along in years is the self-inflating air mattress. Its name is a little misleading; it is actually an open-cell sleeping pad of about ½-inch thickness, enclosed in a waterproof, leakproof nylon cover. A small valve is opened and air enters to fill the open cells of the pad. The valve is then closed, trapping the air inside the cells. The air is not free enough to get very cold, while the high loft of the pad gives the sleeper a high degree of compression comfort.

To roll this device, the valve is again opened and the pad tightly rolled from the foot toward the valve, thus squeezing the air out. Once tightly rolled, the valve is closed and the roll will stay in a compact bundle for carrying.

The self-inflating air mattress provides the advantages of both air mattress and pad, with none of the drawbacks of either. The pad is a bit expensive (up to $30), but there are a great many hikers who would sleep on nothing else—and that number is growing every season as more campers try them.

There are other kinds of less efficient pads and mattresses around, but you probably wouldn't be interested in suffering through the night on any of them. Of those covered here, the air mattress is the least efficient for all-around use, although it can be fine in fair, warm weather. If you carry one, be sure to get a small accordion-style pump to inflate the thing. If the air mattress is large enough to provide summer comfort, you might hyperventilate from inflating your lungs. Cots are about out for the majority of us, and the foam pads or excellent self-inflating pads will be chosen by most of us. Either one can increase the inside temperature of the bag by ten or so degrees.

Nesting Bags

Another way to increase sleeping comfort in the trail camp is to have a second sleeping bag inside the main bag. In most winter camping, the lined tent and pad will give all the comfort necessary, but when things are *cold,* it's nice to have the inner bag. For moderate conditions, a loose flannel bag can be fashioned at home and tucked inside the regular bag.

The flannel bag should be made fully as large as the inside dimensions of the sleeping bag, even though a few folds and wrinkles are going to be created. The air space between the inner and outer bags helps keep the sleeper warm, and even the random folds and wrinkles trap body-warmed air for added insulation.

Under Arctic conditions you might want to tuck a down-filled mummy bag inside the outer bag for added protection. It isn't the freest form of sleeping, but it sure as heck is warm. On a particularly cold night on the Yukon, I put a two-pound mummy bag inside my four-pound down backpack bag and slept very comfortably. The outside air temperature was -56° and it wasn't a lot warmer inside our tent. In the nested sleeping bags, however, it was even a bit warmer than I desired.

Clothes for Wearing to Bed

Finally, you can increase the effective temperature inside the bag by choosing the proper wardrobe for sleeping. The proper attire, incidentally, does not include the outer garments used on the trail, mukluks, or parka. You should undress at least a little before hitting the sack. During cold spells, it is a good idea to wear thermal "fishnet" underwear, perhaps a sweatshirt if you really need it, and a pair of clean, heavy socks. They will give you some added insulation and comfort.

By all means, wear a hat to bed when it is cold. Very few people realize how much heat their scalp dissipates during the night, and many campers sleep cold just because they didn't think to wear a warm cap. A knit cap, similar to the surplus navy "watch" cap, is perfect.

Campers so dressed for bed certainly won't win any fashion award, but they won't shiver their bottoms off either. Admittedly, a few outdoor-oriented newlyweds have had second thoughts after seeing their apprentice spouses attired in sloppy thermal underwear, loose woolen socks, and a knit cap worn at eyebrow level, but they presumably sleep well!

Sleeping with a Friend

Sleeping with a friend is often warmer, provided that zip-together bags have been brought along. This rather social technique might increase the inside temperature by several degrees.

Actually, the devices used for increasing the sleeping temperature discussed so far in this and the preceding chapter follow a pattern of diminishing returns. Each of them, *alone,* will help the situation as indicated in the following chart, but it's absurd to think that their cumulative warming effect will be the total of their individual warming effects. If such were the case, this would be the approximate result:

Outside temperature	51°
Inside the tent (+10°)	61°
Adding a tent liner (+10°)	71°
Sleeping pad (+10°)	81°
Nesting mummy bag (+15°)	96°
Thermal underwear, etc. (+15°)	111°
Friend's body heat (+15°)	126°

Fooey! That would be like trying to sleep at the Magic Fingers Sauna!

Net Hammocks

There is still one more sleeping device to consider strictly as an accessory to the standard camp—the net hammock. When camping conditions become tropical in nature, the new net hammocks are a very comfortable and pleasant alternative to the tent-and-bag combination.

Made of strong nylon netting, some of the more sophisticated hammocks include a surrounding mosquito netting wall and a waterproof roof. The simplest are just a narrow net into which the camper and his sleeping bag are stuffed. Both can be a pleasant departure from the normal sleeping arrangement, but they are a summer-only alternative.

STOWAGE ARRANGEMENTS

There are any number of accessories that can improve the variety of activities around the camp; most of them relate to improving the space available under inclement weather conditions. If, for example, the party is socked in for 3 days by a gully-washing rain, it becomes a trifle tiresome to play 860 consecutive hands of whist while jammed amongst all the gear, foodstuff, and rolled sleeping bags. The ideal answer is to store the unused equipment in an out-of-the-way spot, yet keep it protected from the rainstorm that caused the whole problem. There are a couple of alternative methods of gear stowage in the long-term or stormbound camp.

The addition of a few sewn-in storage nets can help the situation significantly with only a little home crafting required. The stowage units are most often sewn into the upper part of the end of the tent, or else are arranged in a long row at the top of the sidewall. These locations are favored because they don't interfere with either activity inside the tent or with the sleeping space on the floor. At one end of the tent, particularly if it is equipped with a vestibule, there is usually more than enough space for the packs and other gear; the net stowage bags keep all the odds and ends available and in plain view.

The alternative to an inside stowage arrangement is the construction of a waterproof nylon "doghouse" to be pitched somewhere near the camp area. Many hikers who take a lot of long-distance trips have accepted the little houses as a better idea than inside storage. The doghouse, about three feet square, can be fashioned at home from a waterproof, coated nylon. It is usually rigged with local trees or bushes as supports, and can be either pegged down or held in place with rocks. Keeping the supplies, and in particular the foodstuffs, a few yards from camp will lessen the likelihood of an unexpected visit from the local animal population. We'll talk a little more about food storage later.

LIGHTS

The question of auxiliary lighting in the camp isn't really a big thing in the midsummer hiking season, but it becomes an important facet of camp life at other times. In the middle of winter along the northern tier of states, darkness comes on at about 4:00 P.M.—earlier when heavy clouds reduce the available light. During those times a reliable source of light is essential to the routine chores of camping. Anyone who has tried to concoct a stew or determine just when the eggs are done by stovelight is intimately aware of the value of auxiliary light. A flashlight is fine for the occasional search for a wayward spoon or the inevitable midnight march to the latrine, but a better light source must be supplied in the camp.

There are quite a number of electric lights available for the backpack camper, but they all have at least two disadvantages in common. They are relatively heavy to carry, and the spent batteries become a disposal problem. Obviously, the used batteries must be carried back out and tossed in one of society's countless receptacles for garbage; they cannot be buried or left in the woods. Those electric devices with rechargeable batteries are the better choice, but they, too, must be carried both ways.

Many more hikers will choose some sort of fueled light, largely because such lights are a bit lighter to carry and are dependable so long as the fuel holds out. They have one distinct disadvantage, however, that isn't shared by the electrics: they can burn down the tent, or worse! More than one serious forest fire has been caused by a runaway candle in camp.

Kerosene and White Gas Pressure Lanterns

The fuel lights range from the old standby kerosene and white gas pressure lanterns to newer canister lights to candles and fitted "french" lanterns. The choice depends on the amount of weight you are willing to carry and the intensity of light you will need. The latter should be the more important determination in selecting a light, since different kinds of camp activities will require greater or lesser amounts of light to accomplish. The party with nothing on the agenda more involved than fixing dinner or playing cards won't need the amount of light required by a group of sketchers or needle-pointers.

The large kerosene or gas lights are very heavy for the backpacker, but they provide tremendous amounts of light. They are quite acceptable for fairly short hikes, but over a long period will consume a gallon or two of very heavy, bulky fuel. In any party on a long journey, the light must be considered a piece of community equipment; the members must share the task of carrying this kind of gear.

Gas-fired lights get very hot, and they must be kept suspended well away from the tent and gear. Most campers suspend them from the ridgeline of the tent, but even that creates some problems. The tent must be pitched with sufficient strength to keep the weight of the lantern stable. Obviously, a tent collapsed around a hot lantern is a catastrophe-in-the-making.

One enterprising party I visited had fitted their lantern with a sharp, two-foot steel spike for support. They had carefully cut a half-inch hole in the floor of the tent near the center, and the spike was firmly driven into the ground to hold the lantern. It reduced the opportunity for unhindered movement in the living area, but seemed a little safer than other methods.

Pressurized-Canister Lights

The pressurized-canister lights are almost as heavy as the gas lights, and have the added problem of spent canister disposal. They provide bright light, but are equally dangerous to the tent and other flammable materials. They should be handled and treated exactly as the gas and kerosene lights are.

Candle Lanterns

Candle lanterns are somewhat safer than the other fueled lights, but not by much. The one safety feature they can claim is that they tend to extinguish themselves if knocked over in the tent. Being a lot lighter in weight, they can more readily be suspended from the ridgeline of a backpack tent, but they are quite low in light output. Many lightweight hikers use a french candle lantern or the equivalent for simple, routine duties around the camp. In the enclosed space of the tent it gives enough light for essential tasks, but isn't quite bright enough for comfortable reading or other activities requiring close vision.

The Carbon Monoxide Danger

One drawback common to fueled lights of any kind—and an extremely important one—is their production of carbon monoxide through combustion. In a relatively airtight tent, especially in chilly weather, the levels of this deadly gas can reach critical proportions. If a kerosene lantern is left burning inside an enclosed, waterproof tent, the accumulation of CO can reach fatal levels in just an hour or less. Whenever a burning light is used, even a single candle, you must provide adequate ventilation.

The choice of a light is just as personal as any other part of your camping equipment, but it is a choice best made on the basis of knowledge. Before you buy a light source, check all the alternatives and determine just *how much* light you will need *how often*. If the party is economical with the energy required to produce light, it might get along with nothing more than a six-volt battle lantern and a couple of pocket flashlights. A larger party might need a big kerosene lantern for the outside cooking area, but get by with much smaller lights inside its tents. As a rule of thumb, I always try to get along with battery lights wherever possible. By and large they are lighter than fueled lights, more efficient than simple candle lanterns, and pose almost no fire threat to the environment.

EQUIPMENT BAGS

One of the little niceties that can make camp more comfortable is the equipment bag. Most often, this is a lightweight nylon bag that you've home-fashioned to specifically fit one particular group of gear. My favorite is a nylon sack in which my nesting pots and frypan fit. Not only does this keep all my cooking utensils in one place, it keeps the inevitable accumulation of soot and fire-dirt from being spread all over my pack, sleeping bag, and underwear. As the gear is cleaned and readied after a trip, the little equipment bags are tossed into the washer in anticipation of the next outing.

You can easily fabricate fitted bags for your eating gear, extra (usually muddy) footwear, soiled clothing, and whatever else you want. I have made mine of different colors and have come to associate the little orange one with my tea, chocolate, and condiments, and blue one with my cooking utensils, and the tiny red one with my razor, toothbrush, camp soap, and hygiene accessories. They keep the tent a little neater and make life correspondingly easier on the trail.

THE DITTY BAG

There is one more bag that demands a little attention, and it's the one I call the "ditty bag." It is really the camp recreation and hobby center, and no trip would be complete without it. You'll eventually stuff the ditty bag with the little goodies that make life interesting for you. In the typical bag we might find a pipe and tobacco, a dog-eared copy of *Sand County Almanac,* a deck of cards, a pocket glass for investigating insects and tiny blossoms, a field guide to the birds, folding pocket chessboard, a small sketchpad and pencils, extra film, a couple of vials for collecting specimens—the list is virtually endless. The ditty bag contains all those things that take the trip out of the ordinary and help while away those lazy afternoons in camp, should any crop up. Once, after hiking a particularly difficult Olympic Peninsula trail to a group of high lakes, we found a party there engrossed in an afternoon game of Monopoly®. From the evident enjoyment the party was getting from it, that bulky game was a pretty important part of their ditty bag. There aren't any ground rules for this enjoyable part of the gear. You just start with a few things you like, and after a few trips it will build itself into a satisfying part of every wilderness adventure.

COOKING AND EATING GEAR

There are a number of pieces of equipment that are quite necessary to the party; they constitute the portable kitchen. The backpack stove, pots and pans, and the various utensils can hardly be considered accessory to the daily meals, but there are some definite "extras" that might be nice out along the trail. I'd consider a couple of small plastic tarps the most important accessory items you could carry. During inclement weather they can be pitched as an outside cover and windbreak for the cooking detail, making meal preparation easier and more efficient. The cover can be strung between some handy trees, the windbreak rigged from that, and the meal whipped up in relative comfort.

Fire-Prevention Devices

The addition of this auxiliary shelter does more than make outside cooking more efficient; it takes foul-weather cooking outside the tent. The risk of fire is very high when you fire up the backpack stove inside the shelter, and a tarp protecting the outside cooking area simply removes the possibility of fire. Many winter groups, of course, cook their meals in the vestibule or even inside the tent, but I really think the construction of an outside cooking area is well worth the extra bother and effort involved.

If you *must* cook inside, you should either equip the tent floor with a zip-open hole so the stove may be set on bare ground, or else have a sheet metal base on which the cooking is done. Two feet of aluminum under the stove really is a boon to safety and convenience, but a large square of local earth is better. You need only cut an L-shaped slit in the tent floor and equip it with corresponding zippers. When inside cooking is required, open it, fold back the flap, and set the stove on the dirt. In an emergency, the dirt can be used to extinguish a small fire from spilled fuel—but such an accident is hardly consistent with good camping practice.

I have carried a folding sheet of aluminum for inside cooking, but have never been very comfortable about it. I find that a couple of six-foot plastic tarps can be rigged up away from the tent for cooking, even in the worst of weather. I might be a nut about fire prevention, but I don't think I'd mind burning the kitchen down as much as having to spend the night sleeping out in the same lousy weather that drove the cooking under cover!

FOOD AND GARBAGE STORAGE

The well-prepared party always brings along the necessary accessory items for proper food and garbage handling in camp. The amount of garbage generated by the average camper has been reduced dramatically in recent years, but there are still a few items that need taking care of. The equipment to do it is certainly "extra" gear, but it sure helps to have it.

A couple of good nylon bags, about a foot square, should be provided to keep the food together on the trip. Equipped with drawstring, the bags allow everything to be taken from the pack at once, reduce the fumbling and searching for dinner ingredients, and provide an easy means for suspending the food at night. In lieu of a home project, small stuff sacks are available at most outfitters that can be used for carrying and storing the party's provisions.

The necessity of keeping food fresh and edible poses little problem. Most backpackers long ago quit carrying such things as fresh meat, fresh vegetables, semisoft cheese, and a side of salted bacon into the woods. If the bulk and mess didn't discourage them, a horde of hungry raccoons and the specter of botulism did. It's just as well. Nowadays we carry freeze-dried and dehydrated foods that are light in weight, nourishing, and require no refrigeration.

Unfortunately, a few of the foods—notably sugar, honey, and chocolate mix—constitute an attractive temptation to the chronically hungry animals. If the party has already been provided with secure nylon food bags, the problem is much simpler. The bags just have to be suspended between two trees, high enough to keep the larger animals away. A couple of hanks of light nylon line will add only a few ounces to the pack, but will do a lot to keep the party well-fed and happy. If the foods, particularly the more aromatic ones, are also wrapped in plastic to keep the scent down, even the mice and other rodents won't be much of a problem.

In a few of the treeless alpine regions of North America there is nothing high enough to hang the food from. The bushes are often so low that the food can be reached by a kneeling porcupine; so an alternative procedure is necessary. It's possible to put the food under some large rocks, but it doesn't help much. Some parties carry a tiny pocket portable radio along, turn it on just loud enough to be heard a few feet from the cache, and leave it playing all night. That helps, but be sure it isn't loud enough to be heard in your own camp or to disturb others. The portable radio as an electronic scare-away technique may not be terribly effective, but there are few alternatives in a land of few trees and many hungry residents.

Under no circumstances should the food supply be left in the pack or (even worse) inside the tent. A really hungry bear won't care much whether the tent cost a fortune—or even whether you are inside it. He'll come and get what he wants and leave you and your gear badly dented in the process!

Garbage is less of a problem in the trail camp. In the first place, there just shouldn't be much of it, and in the second, you really don't care if some animal eats it or not. You might be carrying out a shredded plastic bag instead of an intact one, but that isn't important. The real reason for keeping the garbage tightly wrapped and out of reach is to keep the animals away in the first place. If they aren't attracted by the more fragrant garbage, they probably won't discover the food cache, either. Garbage is best wrapped tightly in plastic and suspended from trees in the same manner as the food.

HEATERS

The normal winter items that would be considered accessories around the shelter have largely already been covered. They include the tent liner, sleeping pads and bed clothes, and light. The remaining item to consider is the auxiliary heating system that is common to most deep-winter camps.

All of these are essentially liquid-fueled, although at least a couple include pressurized butane or propane cylinders. Either style burns a huge amount of fuel; so carrying them will be something of a task. Vehicular campers will undoubtedly use these portable heaters, some of which have evolved into veritable furnaces.

A stroll through any large outfitter's shop or a glance at the catalog will show you how many different heaters are available. The choice will just be one of how much heat you need, how many days it will be in use, and what fuel you are willing to struggle with. After that, just scrape up the cash and you have the heat source. You've noticed by now that I have ignored the open fire as a source of light or cooking heat. I'm going to ignore it for body heat, too! There are going to be many times that you might be able to use a fire for any of these purposes, but the day of the unrestricted fire has passed. The sooner we all get used to carrying our own fuel and using a *controlled* flame, the better the chances for a perpetual wilderness.

Ventilation Requirements

Whatever auxiliary heater you choose, remember that the production of carbon monoxide is dangerously high in all of them. Some manufacturers of catalytic units claim that the CO developed by their devices is lower than radiation heaters, but don't believe it. You can get just as dead using their heaters as you can anyone else's, so proceed with caution.

It might sound contradictory, but when you heat the

tent with any fueled heater, you must provide a steady supply of fresh air. In fact, the vent system needed for efficient and safe operation of the heater will keep the tent just as cold (or even colder) as if you were to shut off the stove and close the air intake. Experienced cold-weather campers use their stove only for a few minutes to take the chill off, and then rely on their own internal heat to keep warm. If you want to bask in 75° warmth on your bed, you had probably best limit your winter vacations to a motel.

HOUSEKEEPING

There are a few handy items that will help keep the camp clean and pleasant. The summer camper might want to haul along a small whisk broom for removing needles, duff, dirt, and squashed insects from inside the tent. The winter camper carries the same device for brushing snow and ice off before entering the tent. Both are right in trying to keep the inside of the tent clean and dry, and both can use a cheap whisk for that purpose. Most outfitters have a small, inexpensive device especially for the tent camp. Other cleaning gear should already be included in the camp supplies. A little warm water on a sponge will remove dried mud, pitch and sap, or other stubborn dirt from inside the tent. The floor, which luckily is fairly easy to clean, is the part of the tent that becomes soiled most quickly. Sooner or later, someone is bound to track the spoor of an errant buffalo into the tent, and without the proper cleaning gear the atmosphere is going to become a little heady!

The camp repair kit should take care of most of the field wear and tear that occurs. Rips in the canopy or flaps can be sewn with needle and thread, and the mosquito netting can also be sewn if it is torn. The floor or rainfly might require a little hemstitching from time to time, or the damage might be repairable with some nylon tape, which should be included in the kit. Keeping the inside of the tent clean and exercising a little care and common sense when pitching or striking will go a long way toward lowering the frequency of field maintenance.

The accessories available for the trailside shelter are myriad and complex but, fortunately, very few of us want or need everything that has been listed in this chapter. It isn't necessary to live the bare, austere life of the underprivileged caveman, any more than we must expect to live under conditions suited for the Shah of Iran. Somewhere in between is the balance that will make every excursion a pleasure; all we need do is decide what we really want—and choose those accessories that will provide it.

CHAPTER 6

Wall Tents, Trailers, and Other Outsize Shelters

The giant canvas shelters of yesterday have not, as one might expect after looking through an outfitter's catalog, gone the way of the two-handed whipsaw or high-button shoes. Those large, heavy canvas castles are alive and well, living in packsaddles, riverboats, and the backs of station wagons. Although they can hardly be considered "trailside" from the back-packer's point of view, the big wall tents and umbrellas are still very much a part of the camping scene in North America.

The hiker and backpacker has undeniably become something of an elitist in the outdoor world, hardly recognizing the needs or habits of a large contingent of recreational campers. This multitude, nonetheless, is experiencing a perfectly valid type of adventure, albeit with luxury and amenities not available to the self-propelled wanderer. It is true that the charcoal-fired barbecue and the six-volt portable television seem a bit incongruous in the wilderness (or semiwilderness) setting, but we simply cannot ignore the great army of people who choose this form of camping.

The large tents might better be considered as *roadside* shelters rather than *trailside* habitats, but at least a few of them are to be found along popular horse trails and waterways in the wilderness. The big tents are the rule, rather than the exception, at trailhead camps and the sprawling national park campgrounds.

Before we join the pseudosophisticated camping elite in condemning the large structures as conspicuous consumption in the backwoods, let's look at the reasons for their continued popularity. After all, the camper chooses his shelter on the basis of his own activity level. For a lot of people, that activity dictates a large and fairly comfortable established camp.

The vast majority of backcountry deer and elk hunters have found the big wall tents and cottage tents superbly suited to their specific needs. One might differ with them philosophically as to the merit of their sport, but for them it is every bit as valid as that of the scene-hungry hiker and backpacker. Fishermen who ply the secluded lakes of the mountains and the far north are often transported to their recreation by aircraft, large boats, or all-terrain vehicles. The camp may serve a large group for several days or weeks, during which an entirely different life-style is enjoyed. It takes a pretty large and substantial tent to meet the demands of a long-term fishing, hunting, or rockhounding camp.

The large tents are best suited to this kind of activity for several reasons, not the least of which is the elbow room they provide for a nonmobile social situation. Another important consideration is the fact that the tent will be transported mechanically; obviously the hundred-pounders can't be backpacked into the area, unless the back belongs to a mule! Under a wide variety of weather conditions the big canvas tents are surprisingly comfortable. They offer good protection from the sun and wind, are often fitted with a giant canvas fly for additional rain protection, and are so large that condensation is no problem at all. For a two-week stay alongside a big lake, if the area is served by at least a rudimentary road, the wall tent is a pretty good choice.

A few years ago I spent an exciting week in central British Columbia fishing the lakes and rivers of the Cariboo. Our base camp consisted of several large wall tents provided by the outfitter. To say that the accommodations were luxurious would be understating the case badly. We slept on mattressed cots, ate our meals from folding chairs and tables, and bathed regularly in a large canvas tub set up for that express purpose. The fishing was terrific, the country delightful, and the experience was unquestionably a rich and rewarding one. The image was not that of the free-roaming backpacker, but that is precisely the point: it wasn't *supposed* to be! It was a totally different kind of wilderness experience, but no less important than that of the ridgerunner. It is a trip I've repeated a great many times, and will continue to do. In truth, I am a confirmed backpacker who thoroughly enjoys the far reaches of the wilderness, but I enjoy the almost-annual outing in the big tent camp just as much.

The vehicular, horseback, or boat camper has almost as wide a choice of tents and features as does the recreational hiker. The big tents come in anything from a standard two-person model to giant Army-surplus kitchen tents that can sleep an entire troop of the Mighty Beavers Boy's Marching Society! Somewhere in that group of canvas biggies is a tent that will suit any family's camping needs. Despite the great variety of individual tents available, most fall within a half-dozen or so basic styles.

WALL TENTS

Probably the most popular of the big tents, wall tents can be as large or as small as the specific need dictates. These are essentially A-shaped configurations with high vertical walls that provide an enormous amount of inside living space. They are often equipped with two sectional wooden poles, connected by thick metal ferrules. Some feature a wooden ridgepole to prevent the immense weight of the canvas from sagging.

Wall tents can be rigged in any number of ways to keep the floor space free of upright supports. Some of the more ingenious methods of pitching the wall tent have been discontinued because of environmental considerations. In some cases, as many as a dozen stout, young trees were sacrificed to erect the tent, a practice that is both illegal and grossly immoral in most parts of the American forest today.

The modern vehicular camper who carries a wall tent will also carry the proper number of manufactured poles and pegs to pitch it in the campground. After all, if you can carry a 300-pound canvas shelter into the camp, it shouldn't be much of a burden to pack along the poles and pegs as well. In terms of living space versus weight, the wall tent is among the best large tent choices the camping party can make.

COTTAGE TENTS

These big devices are probably the epitome of large-tent camping, and the last word in outdoor luxury. A few models have separated sleeping and eating

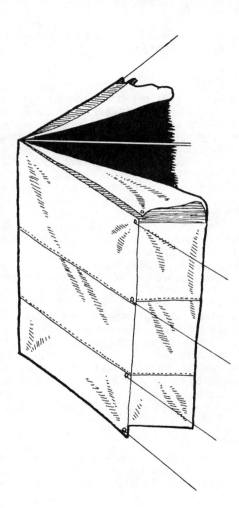

Wall tent.

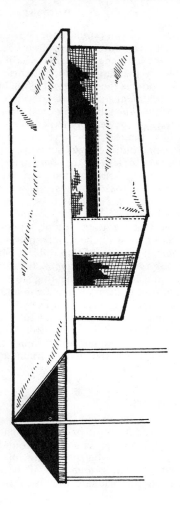

Cottage tent.

quarters, a screened sun porch, and a covered lounging area outside. The cottage tents aren't particularly
prominent on the camping scene, but you'll likely run
into a couple in the larger, more luxurious campgrounds. They look as though a great white hunter will
emerge at any moment to lead his safari into the bush
after mighty Simba, the killer lion of Kalahari.

The cottage tents are terribly expensive, but are an
excellent choice for the very long-term base camp.
Several guides and outfitters will set two or three up at
their operations base, leaving the shelters up the entire
season. Their clients are the kind who expect—and
get—broiled steaks, tossed salads, and clinking iced
drinks in the evenings. Needless to say, they can afford to pay the bill.

Probably the finest cottage tent is a two-bedroom
model with a separate kitchen, screened sun porch,
and an aluminized fabric roof that reflects heat or cold
away from the pampered occupants. It has asbestos-
lined holes for the cooking and heating stove pipes, an
enclosed wardrobe to keep clothes fresh and pressed,
and provision for a rubberized bathtub. It also takes
four strong men, a mobile crane, and a structural
engineer to get it set up properly! Still, some of the
smaller cottage tents could be a comfortable and
manageable choice for the luxury-oriented camping
party.

UMBRELLA TENTS

These are medium-weight tents that will comfortably accommodate from two to four campers. A
few old inside-pole models can still be found, but the
vast majority of umbrella tents are of the outside frame variety. The center pole, if the tent is so
equipped, has the unfortunate drawback of severely

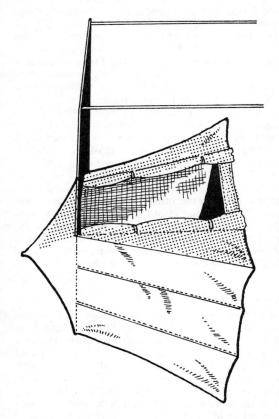

Umbrella tent.

limiting both headroom and living space inside. The outside frame tents, however, leave the inside quite uncluttered and roomy.

Most umbrella tents are constructed of waterproofed cotton drill, about 6- to 8-ounce weight, and may be provided with an optional rainfly. The average umbrella tent weighs no more than forty pounds, often less, and can be lugged with some difficulty to a tentsite quite a distance from the road.

The umbrella tents, because of their desirable ratio of weight to room and comfort, are a favorite of canoe travelers and car-campers. They are carried in a canvas bag about the size and shape of a navy duffel, and can actually be packed quite easily in a boat or sedan.

The camping family on a rather limited budget and not accustomed to the utmost in outdoor luxury will probably find this the ideal choice among the heavyweights. Smaller models will handle two cots easily, three with a little room to spare, and even four cots in a state of chaos. They are priced from about $50 to as much as $200, depending on size and quality.

PYRAMID TENTS

The pyramid tent, in reality an adaptation of the very efficient Indian tepee, has a large contingent of followers in the mobile camping fraternity. Pyramid tents have limited headroom, but provide an awful lot of floor space in relation to overall size. They've been used for many years by such semiprofessional campers as sheepherders and prospectors. The larger pyramid tents are a common sight in the scattered gold prospecting fields of Alaska; their shape tends to shed rain and snow more readily than most other tents.

Pyramid tents share one disadvantage with the um-

Pyramid tent.

brella designs in that a center pole severely restricts the usability of the inside space. Most often they are pitched with a rustic outside frame or suspended from a large limb. At least one model is available with an aluminum four-cornered outside frame.

A handful of traditionalists will probably continue to use the pyramid tent for ages to come, but many people will choose a small wall tent or an umbrella for the greater space-to-weight ratio they offer.

BAKER TENT

The baker tent is a modified lean-to on which the front wall is raised to provide an open-air cooking and lounging area. In the case of inclement weather the wall can be lowered to act as a large door, enclosing the living area against wind and rain.

Originally, the baker tent was designed to allow a reflecting fire to heat the interior (hence the name, likening the tent to a reflector oven), but the restriction that has been placed on open fires in most areas has reduced the advantage of that design feature.

The baker tent is fairly heavy for its interior size, and is almost impossible to fit with an auxiliary rainfly. The open design obviously removes any chance of inside condensation; so most baker tents are constructed of a fully waterproofed canvas drill.

The baker tent is one of the dinosaurs of the tent world, having really outlived its usefulness in modern camping society. Undoubtedly a few diehard traditionalists will take issue with that statement (particularly those who still own and use a baker!), but very few camping families will choose this rather outdated design for their needs. There are just too many roomier, lighter, and less expensive rigs around.

EXPLORER TENTS

This final design is even less suited to modern camping than the preceding model, but there are a few such relics still available in some of the catalogs. There is probably a small demand for them, but it would appear that they are purchased more on the basis of fond recollection and whim than on the purchaser's rational determination of his camping needs.

The explorer tent somewhat resembles a pyramid, except that the highest point has moved from the

Baker tent.

center of the floor space to the front entrance. It allows a stand-up entry into the tent, but you'd better start ducking immediately; the slope drops quickly to the back.

Among the disadvantages of this antiquated design is the tendency of the shallow back slope to quickly collect rain or snow, which in turn bears down on the sleeper at the rear of the tent. If the sleeper is on a cot, a rather common practice among big-tent campers, he makes abrupt and often uncomfortable contact with the tent when he sits up in the morning. If an overnight rain has left the tent cold and clammy, it's a rather rude awakening.

The advantages of the explorer over other tents are hard to find. It is *slightly* lighter than an equivalent umbrella, but hardly enough to notice.

TENT TRAILERS

In the past thirty years the nation's campgrounds have been overwhelmed with an odd assortment of wheeled shelters that include camping trailers, pickup mounted camping bodies, and lightweight tent trailers. The last-mentioned wheeled shelters are mentioned here only because of their superficial resemblance to other large canvas shelters; they are so limited in application that we'll discuss them very briefly.

The tent trailer has been described as the "poor man's camper," a reference to the astronomical price tags on the hard-shelled camp trailers, but to consider a tent trailer costing upwards of $1000 as the poor man's *anything* is rather silly; the cost is just a little lower than some more luxurious trailers.

The site limitation of a tent trailer is probably its greatest disadvantage. The tiniest of the tent trailers must be parked on or near a fairly firm roadway, much

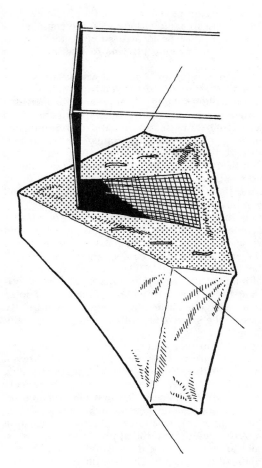

Explorer tent.

nearer the noise and exhaust of the thoroughfare than
most of us care to camp. Along with the camper and
camp trailer, it must be located so close to the busy
highways that it is really little more than a portable
motel.

Many camp trailers are equipped with luxurious accessories that rival the better roadside motel units,
some even having folding TV antennae, flush toilets,
four-burner gas ranges, and propane refrigerators to
keep a case of beer perfectly chilled. Any resemblance
to camping has been carefully eliminated by the manufacturers of tent trailers. Before you start casting
blame on the manufacturers for these garbage-generat-
ing abominations, remember that they wouldn't be
producing them unless there were people ready and
willing to buy them!

Even though the camper equipped with a tent trailer
has become notorious for leaving junk, garbage, and
his own wastes behind, the backpacker, canoeist, and
even the all-terrain vehicle camper should be thankful
that the trailers exist. The users of the tent trailers
have eliminated themselves from competition for off-
road campsites by the narrowness of their own choice
and their insatiable desire for creature comfort. By
comparison, the safari-style cottage tent party is really
"roughing it."

It is a fact, however, that there are some people who
would never learn to appreciate the wilderness (even
the margins) if they weren't able to bring everything
along in the tent trailer. Those who feel such campers
should have stayed home in the first place should remember that tent trailer campers can be the most vocal
and influential people when new wilderness legislation
is being considered. The radial-ply experience is no
less valid to them than the deep woods experience to
the dedicated backpacker. By its affluence alone, the

organized tent-trailer-and-camper crowd has been a significant factor in expanded recreational opportunities for everyone.

There is no point in trying to compare features of the tent trailers so a choice can be made. The models are enlarged and allegedly improved every season. Most of them have luxury accessories in direct proportion to the price; so the choice is more often dictated by one's bank account than by comparative features.

ADVANTAGES OF VEHICULAR CAMPING

The vehicular camper, either wheeled or water-bound, has the option of carrying just about anything he wants into the camp, and the recreation industry has responded by catering to his every whim. Actually, many of the pleasures available to the large-tent camper are beneficial to his safety and enjoyment along the way. Perhaps the most notable difference between the self-propelled and vehicular party is the choice of foods and cooking techniques. The insulated ice chest has given the latter group the option of fresh meats and vegetables, fresh milk and other highly nutritious foods, and a variety that is a practical impossibility for the backpacker.

The methods by which the foods are prepared are also more varied when weight is no longer a consideration. The large tent crowd can have its eggs sunny-side-up, freshly chopped hash brown potatoes, and breakfast sirloins sautéed in burgundy. A few miles away the backpacker may thoroughly enjoy his flapjacks and reconstituted scrambled eggs, but the meal must pale by comparison. Fortunately, people and their tastes are just as different as the breakfasts described, and everybody finds a special satisfaction in his own pursuits.

The vehicular camper can carry all the lanterns and fuel needed to light up the camping area brightly, and he can transport the utensils needed to do practically every little task around camp with ease. He can also bring along all the fishing tackle needed for a variety of conditions, and is able to ice and carry home an immense number of trout or other game fish. All these things can be a boon to the camper, but they must be done with a greater concern for the surroundings than is exercised by the backpacker. The party that carries everything on its backs has neither the inclination nor the physical ability to chop down a giant hemlock for firewood. For the same reasons, the footbound party will take only those trout that it can eat in camp, releasing the remainder of its catch for a future day. The backpacker, by his nature and the limitations he has imposed upon himself, has a less adverse impact on a fragile environment. The horse camper or other heavyweight camper must exercise greater control over himself and his party if his portion of the wilderness is to survive.

In the final analysis, the party that requires the luxury of a mounted or vehicular camp is enjoying a different kind of wilderness experience. This type of camping experience is augmented by literally tons of special supplies and accessories, but differs from the elite hiking party's only as a matter of degree. Those of us who are more involved in the high trails and the deep forests of the pure wilderness can probably never appreciate the large tent camp. We make little, if any, effort to even tolerate the horse party or car campers that we consider less "pure" or "hardy" than ourselves. Nonetheless, theirs is a different kind of experience that they will defend just as vigorously as we do ours—and that's the way it should be!

CHAPTER 7

Emergency Shelters

Through the experience of the survivors of dire tragedy we have learned much about the human body under a variety of adverse conditions, and we've learned how to put a protective shield between ourselves and the silent dangers of the wilderness and the weather. In some cases the bitter lessons—lessons that were purchased at a fearful price—have come after investigating an unsuccessful survival attempt.

The modern hiker is seldom faced with a life-or-death emergency, but a situation can occur in just minutes that changes an outing from a pleasant stroll to a potentially fatal ordeal. The hiker must be prepared, through knowledge and understanding, to deal with the crisis when it occurs.

Most modern survival experts agree that three elements are essential to survival. They are a positive mental attitude, protection from the elements, and water. With these three elements—and no others—

parties have survived long and incredibly painful ordeals.

In the not-too-distant past, most survival manuals dealt almost exclusively with methods of providing food and water for the party. Page after page was devoted to weaving gillnets for fish, building pits, snares and deadfall traps to catch game, and identifying and cooking mushrooms and wild greens.

Those old manuals were fascinating reading and a fine mini-course on early-day woodcraft, but were about as pertinent to the actual survival situation as leaky galoshes. Most paid little attention to the emotional state of the distressed party, only casually discussed the importance of potable drinking water, and dismissed entirely the construction of a temporary, overnight shelter.

In practice, the lost party in North America is rescued (or finds its way home alone) within the first four days after being identified as missing. The great majority of survival situations are resolved within two days. On the rare occasion when a party survives for many days or weeks, it makes headline news, and well it should. The long-term survival ordeal is so rare as to be practically nonexistent. But even for the short haul, the survival requisites of a positive mental attitude (PMA), adequate shelter, and water are more important than all the food-gathering techniques on earth. Modern nutritional science agrees that most healthy adults in reasonably good physical condition can survive for as much as two weeks or longer without any food. A daily intake of water, however, is essential to the maintenance of health in this emergency. Shelter and a PMA are the only requirements needed to protect the physical body from outside damage and hypothermia, and to make the rescuers' job easier by maintaining a vigorous mental and emotional attitude.

Although we have conceded that food is not essential to the maintenance of health for quite a period of time, we must admit that food is a helpful factor in developing and holding a positive outlook in a grim situation. In tests run at military survival schools, student-survivors who were able to forage enough food for at least a perfunctory daily meal quickly adapted to their circumstances and proceeded without difficulty. Those who, through food prejudice or lack of knowledge, went without the daily meal were prime candidates for a terrible experience. The food, it seemed, was a significant contributor to a positive mental attitude.

The hiker facing a survival situation will likely not have a problem with food, unless the emergency lasts for several days. Any person in the wilderness by choice should have carried enough food to last for the planned period and at least a few meals extra. By careful use of the available food, he should be able to provide for himself the essential confidence-building meals.

By the same token, a hiker will almost assuredly have brought along at least minimum shelter with his other gear. It is entirely possible, of course, that the person has somehow become separated from the rest of the party and is lost without a usable tent or tarp. In that case, the survival elements of PMA, water, and shelter will all have to be obtained from the materials at hand. Since this book deals primarily with shelter, it logically follows that our emergency concern will be with providing basic protection from the elements. The other techniques essential to survival should be learned from appropriate sources before planning a long ramble.

WHY THE NEED FOR EMERGENCY SHELTER?

In a large percentage of the actual survival situations encountered in North America, the party has been put in danger by one or more of three factors: (1) a debilitating injury to one or more members of the party, (2) the loss of direction and familiar landmarks, and (3) the sudden development of stormy or cold weather. An emergency can exist even if any one of these elements is missing. Sometimes a sudden change in weather alone can create a potentially disastrous situation.

Accidents to members of the party can occur in every terrain. An accident may mean that the injured person will have to be sheltered and protected while some party members go for help. In that case, either the stationary or the mobile portion of the group may need to use emergency shelter. If a small tent is available, it should be used for the travel party's protection. The rustic shelter can be constructed more efficiently by the larger group at the injury site, and a new source of shelter will not have to be found each night by the travelers. In this way, the rescue group can hike until nearly total darkness, and not have to stop earlier to find and build a shelter along the trail.

If the party is lost, it must decide whether to find its own way out, or to sit tight and wait for help. If someone knows you are missing, it is often better to wait for help. In this circumstance a strong and dependable shelter can be constructed. If the party decides to travel, it will have to use small, temporary shelters wherever it can find them.

TARPS, PONCHOS, AND CAGOULES

In the emergency situation it is essential that the party leader take a calm, accurate inventory of the materials at hand that might be used to protect the party. Any large, waterproof material in the packs could contribute considerably to the shelter. Such hardy garments as ponchos, cagoules, space blankets, and plastic tarps could be all that is needed for an overnight fly. Even a couple of deflated air mattresses could be pressed into service in an emergency to protect the hikers.

Not long ago we talked with a couple of young men who had endured a week of hiking on Washington's Olympic Peninsula, noted for its damp and windy weather. They had become separated from a larger party and had no food, water, or tent. To combat the chill, they dressed in their raingear each night (even though it wasn't raining), spread a small plastic tarp over themselves, and slept in the leeward protection of large logs. They certainly weren't particularly comfortable, but their raingear kept them dry and relatively warm, warding off the hypothermia that would have inevitably come from sleeping on the damp ground. When rescued, they were in excellent condition and fine spirits. They were fully prepared, if the weather became worse, to build a fairly stable shelter from local materials and the space blanket.

A tarp or space blanket can be worked into any number of useful shelter combinations. We've illustrated just a few ways to rig a tarp, poncho, or other waterproof material, but the final design is purely a matter of common sense and using anything around for supports.

When looking for a suitable cover, don't forget that small pieces of plastic, rain jackets, and even garbage sacks can be sewn together with your backpack sewing kit to provide at least a roof over your head.

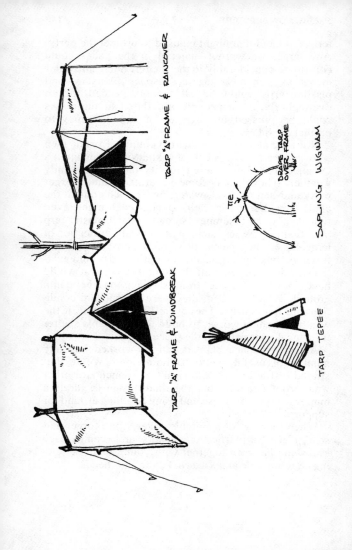

TARP "A" FRAME & RAINCOVER

SAPLING WIGWAM

TIE

DRAPE TARP OVER FRAME

TARP "A" FRAME & WINDBREAK

TARP TEPEE

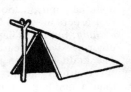

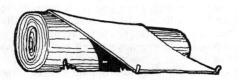

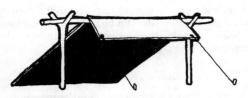

PRIMITIVE TARP SHELTERS

ELTERS FROM NATIVE MATERIALS*

In almost any region of North America it's quite possible to build an adequate shelter using only native materials and no tools whatsoever. It is unthinkable that a person would be caught in the wilderness with *nothing,* but it has happened. For that reason, if for no other, it's wise to carry a pocketknife on your person. The knife has been judged the most valuable single survival tool, and practically every person with more than a nodding acquaintance with the forest carries either a sheath or folding variety.

Caves and Rock Overhangs

The simplest of all the natural shelters is a cave or stone overhang. Unfortunately, such shelters are usually never around when you need them. A really secure and established cave, moreover, usually already has an occupant. The rock overhang is a more common possible emergency shelter, but it will require at least a little help before it provides the proper degree of shelter. The outcropping can be assisted with a couple of very rudimentary walls composed of stones, large saplings, and a covering of boughs.

Lean-tos

A very elementary lean-to can usually be fashioned from the same materials. If a large log can be found, it provides not only the supporting member of the shelter, but a fine wall and an excellent reflector for a

---

Note: The shelter techniques listed here necessarily harm the environment. They require, in many cases, cutting live trees and the use of other plant organisms to the temporary detriment of the wilderness. Under no circumstances, *other than a genuine emergency,* should these techniques be practiced in the forest.

fire. Obviously, the fire should be carefully controlled so the log—and subsequently the shelter—won't burn down, adding to the danger of an already hazardous situation.

The actual configuration of the shelter will depend entirely on what materials are available and how hard you want to work on it. If there are three or four people in the party, it is a good idea to make a fairly secure shelter with more than the average amount of effort. Not only will the task provide the essential protection, it will give the party a very healthy sense of self-confidence. The actual work might be more than really needed, but the labor will help generate internal heat, reinforce the PMA of the party, and develop a spirit of teamwork that could be vital in the days to come.

How to Use Trees, Logs, and Saplings

The standard materials, such as saplings, small logs, and leafy boughs, can easily be augmented by whatever special items might be found. In many older forests there are large wooden slabs from "blowdown" trees, sluffed layers of bark that can make very tight, neat coverings, and fine driftwood materials in the streams. Don't overlook such obvious coverings as palmetto fronds, the tough stems of vine maple, or large leaves such as thimbleberry, maple, and cow parsnip. The large leaves can be overlapped in shingle fashion to help waterproof the roof you've constructed.

Thick stands of conifers, particularly in second growth or old burns, will provide a high degree of protection under the lower branches. In especially heavy thickets you might "carve out" an excellent shelter, well protected from wind and rain. A warming fire under the trees, however, might result in an enveloping forest blaze.

Adaptations of the Wickiup and Tepee

If the party feels that the duration of the stay will be several days, it might be well to construct a really sophisticated native shelter. This is usually done in the manner of the early Indians, construction practices following the extremely efficient methods used for centuries. The illustrations earlier in this chapter show several wickiup and tepee modifications that could be useful in the survival ordeal. These shelters are actually more suited to a week-long stay than to a temporary overnight stop.

The Dugout

Another very efficient and useful shelter for the long haul is the dugout, a modification of the simple lean-to. The shelter requires the use of a shovel, but one can be whittled from a dried chunk of a blowdown tree or driftwood. If you do fashion a rustic shovel, harden it by putting it into an open flame until the wood just begins to char. Scrape the ash away and repeat the process until a very hard edge has been produced.

With the shovel, the sod and dirt removed from the hole can be used for side and front walls. The roof should be a lattice of limbs and saplings woven for stability and covered with many layers of green boughs, green leaves, and anything else that is handy. It's quite possible to build a shelter that can be used quite comfortably for several days or weeks. Actually, it is almost as good as the permanent homes of some of our pioneering ancestors.

If the dugout is chosen, leave one corner of the roof open for a firepit. It is nice to be able to close it during heavy rain, but the shelter with just an open fire area will still offer a high degree of protection. Cooking and heating can be accomplished with a small, hot fire that produces little smoke.

In primarily desert regions, it is difficult to make any kind of shelter without at least a few man-made materials. A shallow dugout is possible, using whatever rocks, sparse scrub, or other supplies can be found. The person lost in a summer desert environment is in dire straits, and needs some very specialized survival techniques that should be learned long before they are actually needed.

The question of winter survival, however, is a much larger one that might easily be faced in practically any part of the continent. There are few places in North America where it never snows, and the less the liklihood of snow, the more likely snow is to be a serious problem. The techniques for finding shelter in such conditions should be reasonably familiar to almost any hiker.

Digging Shelters in Snow

One of the advantages a heavy snow offers in building an emergency shelter is that the material that caused the problem can be part of the solution. The snow that you must be protected from can be—and is—a logical part of the shelter you'll need.

One of the very easiest methods of finding protection in the snow is to dig into the depression on the leeward side of a large standing tree. From that base it is fairly easy to scoop out a space large enough to provide shelter, firmly pack the sidewalls and ceiling in place, and insulate the party from the snow with boughs, a sleeping pad, or anything else at hand. It is a good idea, while you are forming the cave, to leave a sleeping "bench" for each person. If a thaw should occur, the resulting water will collect at the lower levels instead of soaking the occupants and their bags, creating a critical hypothermia hazard and greatly reducing the chance for survival.

The winter shelter might be dug into the side of a fairly firm snowdrift or the side of a shallow hill. The proper site, under these circumstances, would not be under a long slope or a cornice that could be triggered into avalanche by a sudden thaw. If this kind of shelter is made, be sure to provide a breathing vent that cannot be covered by an overnight snowfall. Even if the entrance is covered, there must be some source of fresh air for the party.

The snow trench, discussed in chapter 3, is fairly easy to make, but requires some tool with which to cut the compacted snow. If a machete or saw is available, tromp down the area where the shelter will be constructed to make a firm, compact surface, and then allow it to refreeze for thirty minutes or so. When the area is good and firm, cut the snow and go ahead with construction. The same technique is used in making the traditional igloo, but there is no reason to go to the trouble of building such a complex shelter unless it must serve for several days.

In summer or winter, try to find the very best available shelter, then improve upon it as necessary for the conditions at hand. The emergency shelter will not be roomy or comfortable by any stretch of the imagination. It is supposed to be the best possible place to protect your party from the elements or other dangers under the worst possible circumstances. Given those facts, there is little doubt that the emergency shelter will be cramped, chilly, and dreadfully uncomfortable. Just remember that a difficult and painful survival ordeal is definitely better than the alternative.

CHAPTER 8

The Tenter's Catalog

As we said when this whole thing started, the proper choice of a field shelter depends largely on the activity level of the camper, the special requirements of his type of sport, and the amount of money he is willing to pay to correctly outfit the trail camp. We looked carefully at the various designs, studied the alternatives, and even thought about camping without a tent. Finally, it's time to put the nitty with the gritty and decide just which one of astonishing array of tents on the market will best suit *you,* the ultimate owner, caretaker, and inhabitant of a very special trailside shelter.

On the pages that follow you'll find a pretty thorough cross-section of the world of backpack and vehicle shelters. Even though a hundred different styles, models, and variations of tents are covered, we have only scratched the surface. There are countless imported tents, large canvas affairs, and other configurations on today's market—far too many to be individually listed in any publication. What's more, new innovations are produced every season; so any all-encompassing list would be obsolete before it was printed. What we have done was to select the best-known models of a large number of reputable manufacturers' lines. Please remember that this catalog is incomplete; we are not necessarily endorsing one particular firm over another, nor do we presume that any given model is better or worse than a competitive tent. What we have done is put together what we believe is the best representative cross-section of a large and burgeoning industry. Virtually any person of almost any camping persuasion will find in this catalog exactly the unit that will fit his own unique needs and desires.

The data herein has been supplied directly by the manufacturer or importer of the tent. The dimensions, materials, and specifications are exactly as they've been given to us and have been passed along essentially intact. We have made a number of comments concerning the utility of several of the tents with which we have first-hand experience. The whole reason for this catalog section is to give the potential tent buyer all of the information that it would take him many months to accumulate independently. If we have left some tents out or included others that don't seem particularly valuable to any person, remember that there are several million hikers and campers around, each with some pretty specific requirements of their own. In this listing we feel sure there will be enough information to allow anyone to make an intelligent choice.

The prices quoted are the general range of each model, but they may vary in different areas and under different conditions. The address of each manufacturer is listed before the tents produced by that manufacturer. Feel free to write the makers for any further information. We have found all of them to be reputable and helpful, anxious to give you the full details on every item they sell. Every manufacturer or dealer listed in this section will correct any defect that might be encountered, and will fully guarantee the quality and workmanship of its products.

The shelters described in this section are often very standard in design, with size, weight, and materials being the major variables. We have illustrated those that depart from the design configurations shown elsewhere in this book. It is recommended that the potential tent-buyer contact the supplier directly for illustrative matter, further construction details, and up-to-date exact prices.

ALPINE DESIGN
6185 E. Arapahoe
Boulder, CO 80303

The ECO Series (2 models)
ECO I 8'L x 5'W x 4'H	**7 lbs. 8 oz.**	
ECO II 8'L x 5'W x 4'H	**7 lbs. 10 oz.**	
Rainfly included

Front, back, floor, and sidewalls are of 1.9-oz. coated ripstop nylon. Extralarge zippered rear window for cross-ventilation. Window and entrance protected with fine-mesh mosquito netting. Erected with 57-inch double-A poles at front and rear. The aluminum poles are shock-corded. Tent has inside storage pockets and is treated for flame-retardancy. Eco II features similar construction but includes a tunnel entrance and sleeve vent for foul weather and high-altitude camping. Both come complete with rainfly, pole and peg set. In blue or orange with yellow canopy.

ECO I about $150 from Alpine Design
ECO II about $165 from Alpine Design

No Strings Attached
8′ 6″L x 6′ W x 4′ H   7 lbs. 15 oz.
Rainfly included

A lineless 3-man tent constructed of 1.9-oz. coated ripstop nylon. Features 63-inch double-A pole erection, self-repairing zippers, completely netted door and windows, shock-corded aluminum poles. The same excellent workmanship as is evident in the ECO series of tents. An elasticized rainguard has been installed over the door and windows. There are roomy storage pockets inside. Easy to pitch and strike, this tent comes in blue or orange with yellow canopy.

About $150 from Alpine Design

Timberline
4′ 4″W x 6′ 10″L x 3′ 7″H   6 lbs. 6 oz.
Rainfly included

The Timberline was specifically designed for all-around (including high-altitude) camping. A roomy 47-inch vestibule provides added living and stowage space. Constructed of breathing ripstop, the tent features screened rear window and door, A-pole front support and I-pole rear support, both shock-corded. Excellent material and workmanship make this a fine

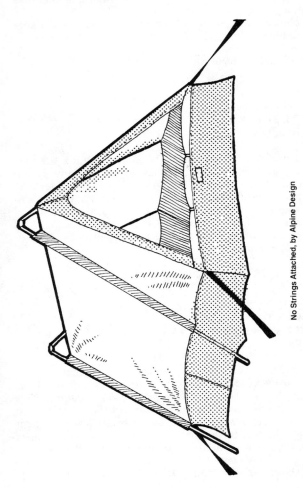

No Strings Attached, by Alpine Design

choice for all-around backpacking. Available in orange
or blue.

About $125 from Alpine Design

Telluride Tent
7' L x 4' 6"W x 4' H   5 lbs. 6 oz.
Rainfly included

Telluride is a high-quality 2-man tent suitable for most
general hiking and camping duties. Canopy of uncoated, breathing nylon taffeta, floor, fly, sidewalls,
and ends of urethane-coated nylon taffeta. Features A-
pole front and I-pole rear supports, self-repairing zippers, netted door and rear window, shock-corded
poles. Comes with rainfly, poles, and pegs. Blue or
orange with yellow canopy.

About $95 from Alpine Design

WIN Tent
7' L x 4' W x 3' 6"H   4 lbs.
Rainfly included

   A relatively low-cost 2-man tent for general hiking
and backpacking. Canopy of breathing taffeta; floor,
fly, and sidewalls of urethane-coated taffeta. This
design uses two I-poles for support, both breakdown
type. Fully netted door and rear window, the light
weight makes this an excellent bicycle tent. Comes
complete with rainfly, pegs, poles, and stuff sack.

About $70 from Alpine Design

ASCENTE
**2126 Inyo Street (P.O. Box 2028)
Fresno, CA 93718**

**Backpacker
7′4″L x 7-2′W (tapered) x 6′H   6 lbs. 5 oz.
Rainfly optional**

This is a double-tapered design that features a very wide front and a low, shallow rear. It is made of ripstop nylon with coated floor and fly. Door is netted with outer flap. No rear window because of low

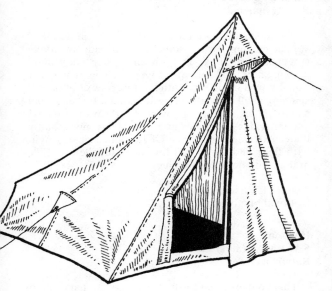

Backpacker, by Ascente

profile. l-pole front and rear supports. The extra height makes this a very comfortable lightweight tent of excellent quality and construction. Comes with tent poles, pegs, and storage bag. Top is green or gold, floor and fly blue.

About $95 from Ascente
Optional rainfly about $45

Expedition
7′ 6″L x 4′ 6″W x 3′ 6″H   8 lbs. 15 oz.
Rainfly optional

An outstanding winter tent, this is a solid double-A-supported tent with screened slit side windows, screened vent tubes at both ends, side snow flaps, cooking hole, and a unique ridgepole. This is an exceptionally well-made tent with reinforcements or double-seaming at all wear and pressure points. It is especially suited to high-elevation, winter, or storm situations and provides a high degree of stability and comfort under extreme conditions. Of 1.9-ounce ripstop nylon with floor and fly coated for water repellency. Sides orange with floor and fly blue.

About $175 from Ascente
Optional rainfly about $30

Horizon
5′ W x 8′ 4″L (max) x 3′ 6″H   7 lbs. 10.5 oz.
Rainfly included

This double-slanted A-frame with a catenary cut top holds two people normally, three in a pinch. Of 1.9-

ounce ripstop nylon with floor and fly coated ripstop. Both ends netted with Velcro® and drawcord vent areas. An excellent quality all-around backpack tent. Canopy green or gold, floor and fly blue.

About $150 from Ascente

Net Tent (MK-2)
7'3"L x 5'W x 3'6"H   5 lbs. .5 oz.
Rainfly included

One of a new breed of tents featuring a netting canopy for "sleeping under the stars" while enjoying plenty of lightweight protection. Floor and sidewalls of coated ripstop nylon, fly also coated nylon. A-pole front and I-pole rear supports. Very light and excellent for summer and fair-weather hiking. Canopy of green or gold, floor and fly blue.

About $90 from Ascente

One-Man Tent
7'6"L x 4'W (max) x 2'10"H   2 lbs. 3.5 oz.
Rainfly included

One of the very few 1-man tents on the market, this design uses the backpack as the major support. Pack contents, obviously, are close at hand. Top is nylon netting, fly coated nylon. A departure from the standard, but an excellent device for the lone-eagle hiker. Green or gold with floor and fly of blue.

About $75 from Ascente

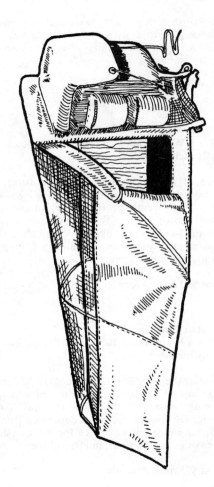

One-Man Tent, by Ascente

Twin Peaks
7' 6"L x 5'W x 3' 6"H   6 lbs.
Rainfly included

A tapered, A-frame 2-man tent of 1.9-ounce ripstop nylon. Fully netted front door and rear window. One of the better all-around tents available, this one features top-quality workmanship and only a moderate taper for added interior roominess. The floor is of coated nylon extending about 8 inches up the sidewalls. The fly is likewise coated nylon. In green or gold with floor and fly of blue.

About $115 from Ascente

L. L. BEAN, INC.
Freeport, Maine 04033

Timberline (2 models)
2-man 5' 3"W x 7' 2"L x 4' 2"H   7 lbs. 14 oz.
4-man 7' 2"W x 8' 9"L x 4' 10"H   9 lbs. 14 oz.
Rainfly included

Bean's better-quality backpack tents for all-around hiking and camping. Constructed of 1.9-ounce ripstop nylon with the same material (coated) for floor and fly. Self-supporting external frames give these tents considerable inside room and comfort. Bean offers an optional storm fly, in addition to the regular fly, that offers excellent winter protection. The storm fly includes a large vestibule area outside the tent proper, added stowage inside the fly at the rear of the tent, and a good insulating air space between the tent and the special fly. Canopy is yellow, floor and fly green.

2-man about $80 (storm fly about $57) from L. L. Bean
4-man about $110 (storm fly about $75) from L. L.
Bean

Bean's A-Type Tent (3 models)
2-man 5'W x 8'L x 3'6"H   8 lbs. 8 oz.
3-man 6'W x 9'L x 5'H   13 lbs.
4-man 7'6"W x 8'L x 6'H   15 lbs.
No rainfly

These low-cost combed poplin fabric tents are really
from the old school of camping, but are fine for the
limited purposes to which they are put. Each features
zippered net doors, storm flaps, sectionalized aluminum poles, and pullouts to add interior room. The
cotton fabric is waterproofed but doesn't "sweat" as
much as a comparable nylon tent. Complete with

Timberline, by L. L. Bean

A-Type Tent, by L. L. Bean

poles, guy lines, and high-impact plastic stakes. Tan color only.

2-man about $34 from L. L. Bean
3-man about $55 from L. L. Bean
4-man about $68 from L. L. Bean

Bean's Alpine Tent (4 models)
2-man 5′ W x 7′ 9″ L x 4′ H   13 lbs. 4 oz.
3-man 7′ W x 8′ 10″ L x 5′ 4″ H   23 lbs.
4-man 8′ W x 10′ L x 6′ 6″ H   30 lbs.
6-man 9′ W x 12′ 3″ L x 6′ 6″ H   33 lbs. 8 oz.
Rainfly optional

Alpine tents in the more traditional style, these are a bit heavy for any but the ruggedest parties (or those with horses). They are made of 7-ounce poplin, with coated nylon floors. Top flies are recommended for foul-weather use. Tents are suspended from a flexible outside frame to provide free-standing stability and comfort. Zippered net door and rear window, separately zippered storm flaps. Tan color with dry finish.

2-man about $75, fly $22 from L. L. Bean
3-man about $115, fly $37 from L. L. Bean
4-man about $160, fly $53 from L. L. Bean
6-man about $180, fly $63 from L. L. Bean

Space Tent (2 models)
No. 10 10′L x 10′W x 8′H, awning 8′ x 10′   43 lbs.
No. 12 11′9″L x 11′9″W x 8′H, awning 8′ x 12′ 49 lbs.
No rainfly required.

This is one of the car camper's delights, a combination wall and umbrella tent with outside frame and a large lounging area. Windows and doors are netted with zippered storm flaps. Sewn-in vinyl-coated nylon floor is flame- and mildew-resistant. Top fly, curtain enclosure, or net enclosure for the lounging area optional at extra cost. An excellent base-camp tent for car or horse parties. Tan with olive green floor.

No. 10 about $180, fly $24, curtain enclosure $40, net enclosure $32 from L. L. Bean
No. 12 about $205, fly $33, curtain enclosure $45, net enclosure $37 from L. L. Bean

Space Tent, by L. L. Bean

Snow Lion Triplex
60"W x 94"L x 44"H   6 lbs. 14 oz.
Rainfly included

An innovative mountain tent, the Snow Lion allows the addition of two 44 x 44-inch snow modules at the ends and has an optional frost shield. The modules have tunnel vents on the sides to allow access from either end. The basic tent has inside storage, snaps for the liner, and A-frame supports. It is made of 1.9-ounce breathing ripstop with 2.5-ounce coated sidewalls, floor, and fly. The snow modules weigh 1 pound 14 ounces each, the liner 1 pound 4 ounces. Canopy is gold, floor and fly blue.

About $144, fly included, from L. L. Bean
Snow modules $35 each, liner $25 from L. L. Bean

Backpacker (2 models)
2-man 5'W x 8'L x 3'6"H   5 lbs.
4-man 7'W x 8'8"L x 6'H   7 lbs. 12 oz.
Rainfly optional

Two rather standard backpack tents of 1.9-ounce ripstop nylon with coated ripstop floors, sidewalls, and fly. Netted rear and side windows, netted door and outside storm flaps. I-pole used at both ends for suspension. Pullouts on each side increase inside room. Complete with poles, guys, and pegs with stuff sack. Orange.

2-man about $48, fly about $21 from L. L. Bean
4-man about $75, fly about $28 from L. L. Bean

Baker
7'4"L x 7'4"W x 6'H   11 lbs.
No rainfly needed

The classic baker design for car or other vehicular campers. An optional screen weighing 3½ pounds is available for the "porch" that provides pest-free lounging or sleeping. The light weight is attained by using 1.9-ounce ripstop nylon, coated for waterproofing. Comes with sectional aluminum poles, guys, pegs, and carrying bag. In green only.

About $80, porch screening $19 from L. L. Bean

Pine Tree (3 models)
No. 10 10'L x 8'W x 7'8"H + 10' x 8' fly   35 lbs.
No. 12 12'L x 9'W x 7'8"H + 12' x 9' fly   42 lbs.
No. 13 13'L x 10'W x 8'H + 13' x 10' fly   51 lbs.
No rainfly required

A classic example of the cottage tents with a large optional fly for lounging, cooking, and other camp activity. Made of 7-ounce poplin canvas, these giant tents are fine for the large family or the established base camp. Obviously, these are for vehicle or boats. Floors are coated nylon, all windows and doors screened. Sectional outside aluminum frames and pegs are furnished. In pearl gray.

No. 10 about $153, fly $41 from L. L. Bean
No. 12 about $180, fly $49 from L. L. Bean
No. 13 about $195, fly $50 from L. L. Bean

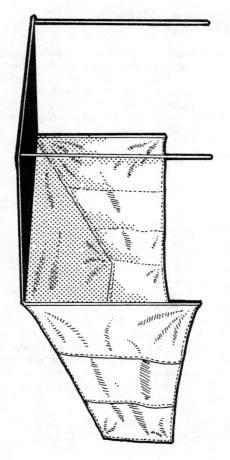

Baker Tent

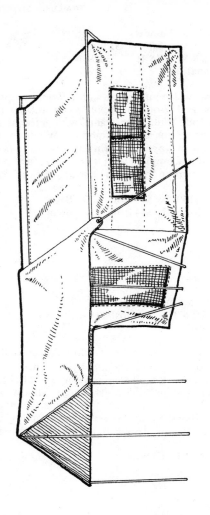

Pine Tree, by L. L. Bean

Bean's Wall Tent (2 models)
No. 10 10′L x 8′W x 7′8″   32 lbs.
No. 12 12′L x 9′W x 7′8″H   36 lbs.
Rainfly optional

The classic wall tent design with 1.9-ounce ripstop nylon walls and 7-ounce poplin waterproofed roof canopy. Outside aluminum frame with internal aluminum ridgepole for added stability. Windows and doors netted with zippered storm flaps. Sewn-in floors of coated nylon. Complete with frame, guys, and pegs. Walls and floor green, roof pearl gray, fly green.

No. 10 about $140, fly $38 from L. L. Bean
No. 12 about $156, fly $44 from L. L. Bean

Improved Nylon Umbrella
9′6″L x 9′6″ 7′7′6″H   24 lbs. 10 oz.
Rainfly included

A modern version of the old standby, the umbrella is constructed of 1.9-ounce ripstop nylon with an uncoated, breathing roof. The fly is fitted and of coated ripstop, as are the high sidewalls. Large windows and door are netted with zippered storm flaps. Complete with outside frame supports, seam sealer, pegs, and carry bag. Floor and walls green, roof gold, fly green.

About $150 from L. L. Bean

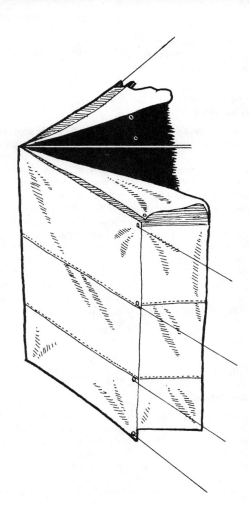

Wall Tent

EARLY WINTERS, Ltd.
110 Prefontaine Street S.
Seattle, WA 98104

Omnipotent
93"L x 54"W x 38"H   5 lbs. 9 oz.
Rainfly included

One of the really amazing departures in design, the
Omnipotent is the first really well-developed tunnel
design on the current market. It is made of two
separate nylon shells suspended by a series of arched
fiberglass supports. The waterproof outer skin is of
2.2-ounce polymer-coated ripstop, the inner shell of
1.5-ounce ripstop breathing nylon. This innovation
features nylon coil zippers, close-weave netting, and
an optional vestibule for added living space. The outer
layer is blue, the inner gold, the netting green, and the
3.3-ounce polymer-coated floors silver gray or sand.
The shock-corded fiberglass supports are joined by
machine alloy aluminum. One of the most stable of all
high-elevation shelters, the tunnel is getting a lot of attention from the all-around hiking fraternity.

About $290, optional vestibule about $30 from Early
Winters, Ltd.

Light Dimension
97"L x 56"W x 39"H   3 lbs. 8 oz.
No rainfly required

The first production model of a shelter made of
Gore-Tex®, a multilayer fabric discussed in chapter 4.
The tent is a smaller version of the great Omnipotent
from the same firm. The essential vaulted arch design
produces a lot of space with little weight, and the use
of the new miracle fabric negates the need for a
separate fly. The material will allow vapor *out* but

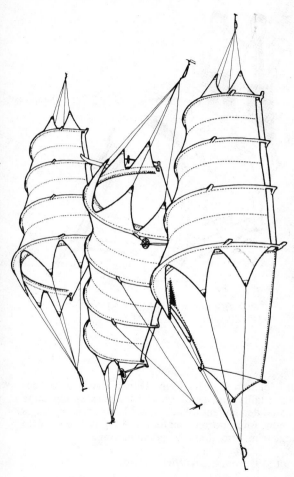

Omnipotent, by Early Winters, Ltd.

Light Dimension, by Early Winters, Ltd.

won't let rain *in*. The Light Dimension is of exceptional quality and stability. It incorporates the same essential design features as its big brother but includes the new microporous material. Acapulco gold with orange trim, gray floor and green netting.

About $195 from Early Winters, Ltd.

EASTERN MOUNTAIN SPORTS INC.
1041 Commonwealth Ave.
Boston, Mass. 02215

Alcove
7′ 6″L x 4′ 8″W x 4′ H   7 lbs. 4 oz.
Rainfly included

An excellent all-season tent of 1.9-ounce ripstop with coated fly, floor, and lower sidewall. A zippered cook hole has been set into the floor, a netted vent is near the peak, and all entrances are fully netted. A 3-sided vestibule has been added for winter use, and a double A-pole support system is utilized. This tent is of outstanding quality and has a lot of well-planned winter features for the price. Floor is blue, canopy and fly yellow.

About $135 from EMS

Kaskawalsh
7′ 6″L x 4′ 8″W x 4′ H   6 lbs. 12 oz.
Rainfly included

An excellent general-purpose tent, the Kaskawalsh is essentially a less-involved version of the same manufacturer's Alcove featured above. It has catenary cut ridgeline, pullouts for added inside space. Workmanship and materials are of the highest order. The double A-pole supports are connected with shock cords and nylon fittings. All openings are fully netted with nylon coil zipper storm flaps. Yellow with blue floor and sidewalls.

About $115 from EMS

EMSKIT Le Manoir
7′5″L x 4′7″W x 3′7″H   7 lbs. 6 oz.
Rainfly included

This is a superb answer to the do-it-yourselfer in all of us. The high-quality backpack tent is a kit, with complete instructions and all materials furnished. The canopy is 1.9-ounce ripstop nylon, floor and fly of 2.5-ounce coated taffeta. All openings (when finished) are netted quite fully, with zippered storm flaps. Double A-pole suspension fully shock-corded. The material selection is superb; the workmanship is up to you. Floor and sidewalls are green, canopy and fly orange.

About $80 from EMS

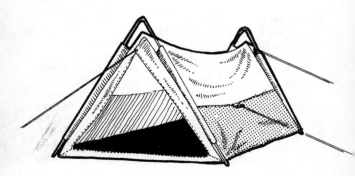

EMSKIT Le Manoir, by Eastern Mountain Sports

Mosquito Net Tent
7′6″L x 4′8″W x 4′H   5 lbs. 6 oz.
Rainfly included

One of the net-sided tents that are growing in popularity for tropical and desert camping. Suspension is A-pole at the front, I-pole rear, shock-corded. The sidewalls are of coated ripstop, fly of 1.7-ounce coated nylon, and canopy of high-grade mosquito netting. Nylon coil zippers on mosquito flaps and storm flaps. No need for windows; the whole canopy is see-through. Fitted rainfly for weather protection and (occasionally) privacy. Tent blue, fly yellow.

About $85 from EMS

EDDIE BAUER EXPEDITION OUTFITTER
P.O. Box 3700
Seattle, WA 98124

Backpacker
5′W x 8′L x 3′6″H   6 lbs. 4 oz.
No rainfly required

A lightweight, coated-fabric tent with 4-way ventilation to minimize interior condensation. It is not designed for extreme cold or high altitudes, but performs nicely under rather routine conditions. I-pole support, fully netted rear and side windows and door with zippered storm flaps. The side windows are protected by wide pullout/storm guards. Complete with aluminum poles, guys, stakes, and carry bag. Green.

About $50 from Eddie Bauer

Trail Tent
7' L x 4' 7"W x 4' H   5 lbs. 8 oz.
Rainfly included

An excellent sloping-ridge 2-man backpacker of 1.9-ounce ripstop. The floor and fly are of urethane-coated nylon. Fully zippered storm flaps cover netted door and windows. A-pole front support, I-pole rear support. Lightweight fly is 1.1-ounce polyurethane-coated nylon. Blue tent with orange fly.

About $95 from Eddie Bauer

Quinault
84"L x 53"W x 48"H   7 lbs.
Rainfly included

The Quinault is a fine all-season tent that can serve a multitude of hiking and backpack purposes. Canopy, ends, and vestibule are 1.9-ounce ripstop nylon. Floor is of 2.2-ounce coated nylon, while fly is of 1.6-ounce coated ripstop nylon. All strain points are reinforced; catenary cut ridge and pullouts help maintain integral strength and generous interior size. Double A-pole supports are shock-corded and fit through channels into base grommets for perfect tension stability. Storage pockets inside, fully netted openings, and zippered storm flaps. Superior quality all-around tent in blue with orange fly.

About $125 from Eddie Bauer

Snowline
98″L x 58″W x 48″H   8 lbs. 11 oz.
Rainfly included

A superior-quality winter tent with an opening vestibule at one end and a tunnel entrance at the other. Has sleeve vents and all openings are fully netted for insect protection. Body of tent is 1.9-ounce ripstop; floor, sidewalls, and vestibule of 2.2-ounce coated nylon. Fly is 1.6-ounce coated ripstop nylon. Wide snow flaps help anchor the tent in deep snow. Double A-pole supports are shock-corded. Zippered cook hole is in the vestibule. All seams are double-needle-felled, reinforced at strain points. Zippered storm flaps throughout. Canopy is yellow, floor and fly green.

About $165 from Eddie Bauer

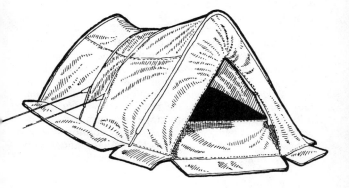

Snowline, by Eddie Bauer

Expedition
**84″L x 60″W x 48″H + 30″and 22″ vestibules   12 lbs.
8 oz.**
Rainfly included, frost liner optonal

A serious piece of equipment for the serious mountaineer, this superbly designed and crafted tent is more
than the average hiker will ever need. Construction is
of 1.9-ounce nylon taffeta, 1.9-ounce coated floor,
aluminum and fiberglass frame, tunneled storm opening and standard storm flap, snow flaps all around.
Used by the 1973 American Dhaulagiri and 1974 Pamir
expeditions. Tent is orange and green, fly orange.

About $225, liner $25 from Eddie Bauer

Overnighter (2 models)
2-man 7′L x 5′W x 3′9″H   11 lbs. 2 oz.
4-man 10′L x 8′W x 5′6″H   23 lbs.
Rainfly included

A fully free-standing outside-frame tent that
provides lots of room and comfort. The canopy is of
1.9-ounce ripstop nylon, the floor, sidewalls and fly
of polyurethane coated nylon. The tent is stretched
with shock cord to maintain proper tension. Door and
rear window openings are protected by overhangs,
fully netted and fitted with zippered storm flaps. This
not-quite-backpack series is especially comfortable as
a base camp for fishing, rockhounding, and other
activity. Pearl green with floor and sidewall of brown.

2-man about $152 from Eddie Bauer
4-man about $225 from Eddie Bauer

Lightweight Family Tent
108″L x 84″W x 72″H   10 lbs. 10 oz.
Rainfly included

A rather large nylon configuration, this tent provides a large vestibule area in the rear and sleeps 4 easily. The canopy is 1.9-ounce ripstop, the floor and fly of coated 1.9-ounce ripstop. All major seams are double-needle-felled; the window and door are fully netted, and have zippered storm flaps. The modified taper of the ridge drops to 54 inches at the rear. Pole arrangement not specified by manufacturer. Floor and sidewalls green, canopy and fly orange.

About $155 from Eddie Bauer

EUREKA TENT AND AWNING CO.
(Available through
Eastern Mountain Sports
1041 Commonwealth Ave.
Boston, MA 02215 and others)

Mount Marcy Tent
7′10″L x 5′W x 3′8″H   5 lbs. 1 oz.
No rainfly required

One of the lightweight backpack tents of coated nylon. Because of condensation when vents are closed, it is recommended for 3-season camping where rain and cold are not common. Aluminum I-poles at both ends. Dealer recommends seam sealant be applied after purchase. Orange.

About $53 from EMS

Nu-Lite 2-man
7' L x 4'10"W x 3'8"H   4 lbs. 2 oz.
No Rainfly required

A very light coated nylon taffeta tent of simple design. Window and door are netted with zippered storm flaps. I-pole suspension at front and rear. Side pullouts for more inside space. Very light and inexpensive, a good novice tent. In tan, olive, blue or green, as available.

About $37 from EMS

Timberline (2 models)
2-man 7' L x 5'3"W x 3'10"H   8 lbs.
4-man 8'10"L x 7'W x 5'2"H   11 lbs. 2 oz.
Rainfly included

These are A-pole-supported shelters of 1.9-ounce ripstop. The floors and flies are of coated 1.9-ounce ripstop nylon, doors and windows are netted and have zippered storm flaps. Self-stabilizing design isn't pegged unless anchors against wind are needed. The fly requires minimum pegging. Zippers are nylon. Excellent quality of materials and construction. Green.

2-man about $80 from EMS
4-man about $116 from EMS

Mount Katahdin (2 Models)
2-man 7'8"L x 5'W x 3'2"H   6 lbs. 9 oz.
3-man 8'9"L x 6'W x 4'4"H   8 lbs. 13 oz.
Rainfly included

Canopy of breathing 1.9-ounce ripstop, floor and fly of coated 1.9-ounce ripstop. Window and door

netted and fitted with zippered storm flaps. l-pole front
and rear supports. Reinforced side pullouts for added
interior roominess. An excellent basic backpack tent
for 3-season comfort. Canopy gold, floor and sidewalls
green. Fly green.

2-man about $75 from EMS
3-man about $96 from EMS

GERRY (Division of Outdoor Sports Industries)
5450 North Valley Highway
Denver, CO 80216

Camponaire II T113
7′ L x 6′ 6″W x 5′ 3″H   9 lbs. 8 oz.
Rainfly included

A roomy, high-center tent of 1.9-ounce ripstop
nylon with 2.7-ounce coated taffeta floor. Fly is of
coated 2.5-ounce ripstop nylon. Inside pockets for
storage, center A-pole and l-pole front supports. Openings are fully netted with secure storm flaps. The
unique suspension is that of the firm's "cross-ridge"
series, which provides lots of inside room for the size
of the tent. Canopy gold, floor and fly blue.

Write for price information

Year-Round II T106
7′ 8″L x 4′ 7″W x 3′ 7″H   7 lbs.
Rainfly included

A gently sloping ridge design, this tent is constructed of 1.9-ounce ripstop with coated 2.7-ounce

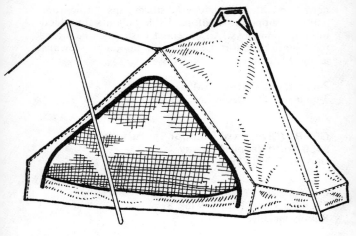

Camponaire II, by Gerry

taffeta floor and 2.5-ounce ripstop fly. A-pole front
and I-pole rear supports, all openings netted and fitted
with zippered storm flaps. The large entry may be used
as a vestibule for foul-weather cooking. Excellent
construction quality and quite roomy. Canopy is gold,
floor and fly of blue.

Write for price information

Fortnight II T114
7′ L x 8′ W x 6′ H   11 lbs.
Rainfly included

Another of the "cross-ridge" series, this tent is of
1.9-ounce ripstop with coated taffeta floor and 2.5-

ounce coated ripstop fly. It uses the unique A-pole center support and front I-pole. Fully zippered storm flaps and net door, netted window. Inside storage pockets, clothesline tabs, and high sidewalls. Includes fly, poles, and stakes. Canopy gold, floor and fly blue.

Write for price information

Southface T150
7'L x 4'6"W x 3'8"H   6 lbs. 10 oz.
Rainfly included

A sloping ridge tent designed for severe weather and wind conditions. Canopy of 1.9-ounce ripstop, floor of 2.6-ounce taffeta. Lightweight fly is 1.5-ounce coated ripstop. Double A-pole supports, fully netted openings with zippered storm flaps. Side pullouts for inside room; all seams catenary cut for stability in wind. Canopy orange, floor and fly blue.

Write for price information

Mountain II T200
7'4"L x 4'6"W x 3'9"H   8 lbs. 6 oz.
Rainfly included

A popular expedition tent with storage vestibule, cook hole in floor, and rear tunnel entrance. Double A-pole supports, finest of materials and workmanship throughout. Fully netted and zippered enclosures allow 2 tents to be joined at the tunnels for a mountaineering base camp. Tent has 1.9-ounce ripstop canopy, coated floors and fly, all seams catenary cut. Canopy orange, floor and fly blue.

Write for price information

Himalayan T230
10′6″L x 5′W x 4′6″H   12 lbs. 12 oz.
Rainfly included, frost liner available

A major contribution to the shelter needs of many high-elevation mountaineering parties. Constructed of 2.5-ounce nylon taffeta with double 2.7-ounce coated expedition floor. Double A-pole support with attached snow flaps and vestibules at either end. Fiber wand glass wall stabilizers and catenary cut seams make this an unflappable, secure shelter under the most difficult of conditions. Cook hole in vestibule for best utilization of inside space. Tunnel entrance can be tied shut for extra stowage. Orange.

Write for price information

Pioneer T421
8′2″L x 6′6′W   Weight not given

A very light tarp tent of coated taffeta with mosquito netting at both ends. A versatile shelter where conditions don't require a full tent. Can be rigged as a 1-man shelter with floor or as a 2- to 3-man cover with a poncho or auxiliary tarp as flooring. No stakes or poles included. Moss green.

Write for price information

Meadow T303
7′L x 4′6″W x 4′H   5 lbs. 6 oz.
Rainfly included

A very lightweight general backpack tent of high quality. Canopy is 1.9-ounce ripstop nylon, floor 2.7-

Himalayan, by Gerry

ounce coated nylon taffeta pulled into high sidewalls
and 3-inch front sill. Fly is of 2.5-ounce ripstop with
urethane coating. All entrances and window fully netted and fitted with zippered storm flaps. Self-locking
aluminum I-pole supports front and rear. Canopy gold,
floor and fly green.

Write for price information

Mosquito T301
7′ L x 4′ 6″W x 4′ H   5 lbs. 6 oz.
Rainfly included

One of the net tents that are growing in popularity
for high, dry camping in many warm parts of the
country. The canopy is no-see-um-proof nylon net.
Floor and sidewalls are 2.7-ounce coated nylon taffeta. Fly is 2.5-ounce coated ripstop nylon. Pullout
sides increase usable inside space. Rainfly can be tied
back on hot nights, allowing a "sleep under the stars"
feeling. Self-locking I-pole supports, moderately sloping ridgeline. Not recommended by manufacturer for
areas of much wind-driven rain. Moss green.

Write for price information

HOLUBAR MOUNTAINEERING LTD.
Box 7
Boulder, CO 80302

Royalite II
7′ 6″L x 5′ W x 4′ 6″H   6 lbs. 14 oz.
Rainfly included

A very popular style of double-tapered 2-man tents,
this one features 1.9-ounce ripstop canopy, 2.7-

ounce coated nylon floor, and 1.5-ounce coated fly of nylon. The suspension is A-pole at the front, I-pole rear, with sidewall pullouts for extra inside room. Mosquito netting door zips open to one side; the storm flap zips open downward. Poles are shock-corded for erection ease. Complete with fly, poles, stakes. Canopy is blue, floor avocado, fly green.

About $135 from Holubar

Expedition
9′6″L x 5′W x 3′11″H   10 lbs. 1 oz.
Rainfly included

A superb high-altitude tent in the upper-medium weight range. It features double A-pole suspension with sectioned shock-corded poles, inside storage pockets, clothesline tabs. Triangular front entrance, tunnel rear entrance, plus sleeve vent, all netted and with zippered storm flaps. Fly is 1.5-ounce coated nylon, canopy of 1.9-ounce breathing ripstop, floor of extraheavy 4-ounce coated nylon to take the beating of alpine moraines. Zippered cook hole in floor. Optional frost shield weighs 1 pound 4 ounces, and snow flaps can also be added for high-wind and snow conditions. Canopy blue, floor camel, fly orange or green.

Chateau
10′5″L x 7′2″W x 5′6″H   10 lbs. 4 oz.
Rainfly included

A novel and fully equipped modification of the vaulted tunnel tent, this model is of 1.9-ounce ripstop with coated 2.7-ounce nylon floor and 1.5-ounce

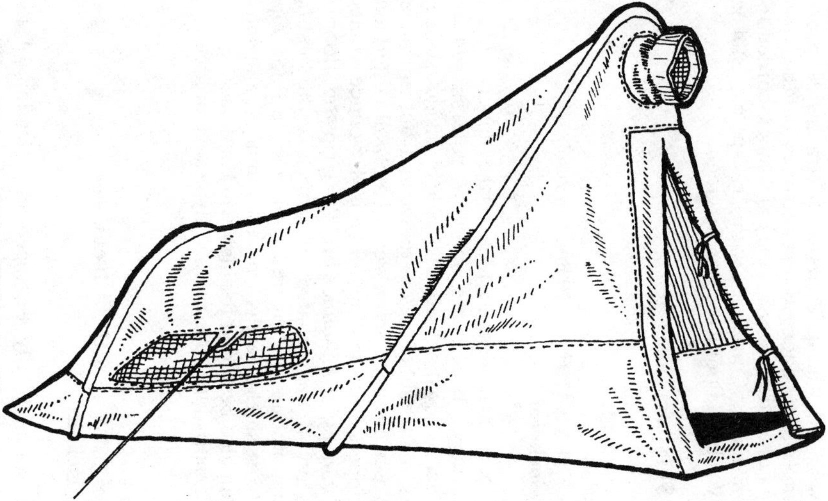

Chateau, by Holubar Mountaineering Ltd.

polymer-coated contoured fly. Curved, external aluminum support system is unique to this model and the slightly smaller companion, the Villa (2-man model). Door, windows, and sleeve vent are netted with storm flaps, nylon zippers. Storage compartments inside with clothesline tabs. Normally secured with only 4 stakes, but provision is made for front and rear plus pullout staking for high wind conditions. A lot of usable free space for the weight. (The smaller Villa is 8 pounds 6 ounces complete.) Both canopies blue, floors avocado, rainfly green.

About $200 (Villa about $175) from Holubar

JANSPORT
Paine Field Industrial Park
Everett, WA 98204

Rover Dome
6′8″W x 7′9″L x 40.5″H   6 lbs. 4 oz.
Rainfly included

The famous Jansport dome has become a familiar fixture along the hiking trails of the world, and all 6 of the firm's tents are essentially this shape. The canopies are of breathing 1.9-ounce nylon ripstop, floors and sidewalls of coated 2.2-ounce nylon taffeta. This model features three mesh side panels for cooling comfort. Fiberglass tension rod supports. Various colors.

About $110 from Jansport

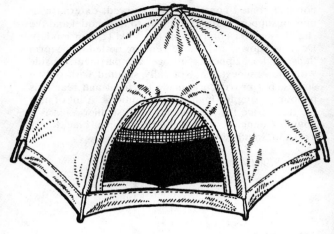

Dome Tent

Trail Wedge
4′5″W x 7′6″L x 4′4″H   6 lbs. 7 oz.
Rainfly included

A modification of the pure dome, this one is light-weight but roomy. Door and vent netted, full storm flaps. Fiberglass supports. Various colors.

About $130 from Jansport

Sun Wedge
4′5″W x 7′6″L x 4′4″H   5 lbs. 11 oz.
Rainfly included

Essentially a variation of the Trail Wedge, with side panels of mosquito netting for added circulation in warm weather. Excellent for predominantly hot or high and dry conditions. With fly in place there is excellent heat retention and circulation. Various colors.

About $120 from Jansport

Trail Dome
7′ 3″ W x 8′ 4″ L x 4′ 2″ H   8 lbs. 11oz.
Rainfly included

Top half of permeable dacron and bottom of coated nylon. Ventilation control through double sliders on doors and toggle drawcord. Storage pockets on inside walls. Spacious and very stable shelter, comfortable for almost all 3-season hiking duties. Can be staked down for high wind conditions. Various colors.

About $165 from Jansport

Mountain Dome
7′ 9″ W x 8′ 4″ L x 4′ 2″ H   9 lbs. 15 oz.
Rainfly included, liner optional

This high-altitude version of the dome features regular triangle door and storm tunnel access on opposite side. Rainfly has zippered access to both entrances, provides excellent insulation air space between fly and tent. Snow flaps may be used to secure in snow. Entrances netted, plus storm flaps. The fiberglass supports allow the tent to be compressed to almost any ledge shape, and tent can be moved without striking if conditions require a quick location change. Can be guyed and staked against severe storm conditions for surprising quiet and comfort.

About $195 from Jansport

Four- to Six-Person Dome
9′7″W x 11′L x 5′9″H   12 lbs. 11 oz.
Rainfly included

A relatively recent addition to the Jansport line, this is the "grand-daddy" of the domes. It provides an inordinate amount of inside space for the weight, and can be very comfortable for the larger party. Standard features as compared with the other Jansport tents, but exceptionally stable and roomy. One of the largest backpack tents available, excellent quality.

About $265 from Jansport

THE NORTH FACE
P.O. Box 2399, Station A
Berkeley, CA 94702

Tuolumne
84″L x 50″W x 56″H   5 lbs. 8 oz.
Rainfly included

A compact 2-man backpack tent with plenty of room. Sloping ridge design, A-pole front and I-pole rear supports. Catenary cut for solid stability when pitched. Side pullouts, sleeve vent, fully netted with tunnel entrance. Roomy and comfortable inside, but smaller than many other of this firm's models. Superb quality throughout. Gold/blue, blue/taupe.

About $135 from North Face

Grasshopper
90″L x 90″W x 50″H   5 lbs. 6 oz.
No rainfly required

Really a novel design, this tent provides an enormous inside space for the very light weight. It is

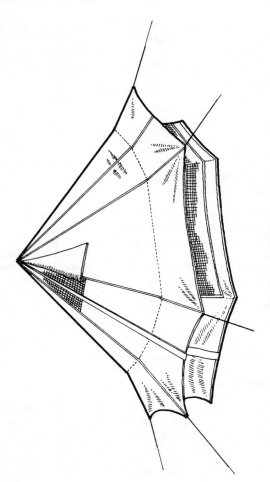

Grasshopper, by The North Face

coated 2.2-ounce nylon, but the size and venting system help reduce inside condensation. The overhang protects the mesh sidewalls that almost entirely circle the tent, further reducing condensation. A single l-pole suspension is used, but pitching is quick and easy. One of the lightest (and cutest) 3-person shelters on the trail. Gold.

About $110 from North Face

Sierra
89″L x 56″W x 56″H   6 lbs. 15 oz.
Rainfly included

A top-grade 2-man backpacker with double A-pole suspension, fully netted door and vent, and zippered storm flaps. Inside storage pockets. Two side pullouts and catenary cut result in wrinkle-free pitching. Snug, overhanging fly. Floor, ends, and sidewalls of coated nylon, with breathing canopy. Gold/taupe, gold/blue.

About $165 from North Face

Mountain/St. Elias
94″ x 56″x 56″H   7 lbs. 5 oz. (Mountain)
**   8 lbs. 6 oz. (St. Elias)**
Rainfly included

Two models, the St. Elias being a modification of the Mountain. Both are double A-pole-supported with side pullouts, all openings netted, zippered rainflies. Both feature catenary cuts, triangle openings at one end, tunneled access at the other, and sleeve vents. The St. Elias also includes a Velcro®-attached cotton frost liner (one of the best around), zippered cook hole in the floor, and permanently attached snow flaps. Mountain is a 4-season tent, St. Elias especially suited to mountaineering and extremely difficult terrain and weather conditions. Both are of superb quality. Mountain: green/taupe or gold/blue. St. Elias: blue/orange, gold/blue.

Mountain about $180 from North Face
St. Elias about $225 from North Face

Oval inTention
114″L x 79″W x 51″H   9 lbs.
Rainfly included

Another dramatic departure from the ordinary, this tent is really a portable geodesic shelter supported by 6 flexible, shock-corded wands. The tent is supported from these by 15 rings mounted in the skin. Because of the unique shape, you can lean back against the walls. The door and 2 windows are zipper-controlled and netted. Full storm flaps. Huge interior space with light weight. Gold/navy or gold/taupe.

About $285 from North Face

Morning Glory
168″L x 96″W x 72″H   13 lbs. 8 oz.
Rainfly included

A really immense and different 4- to 5-person tent, this model gives great space at relatively light weight. It is erected with a center A-pole and end I-pole con-

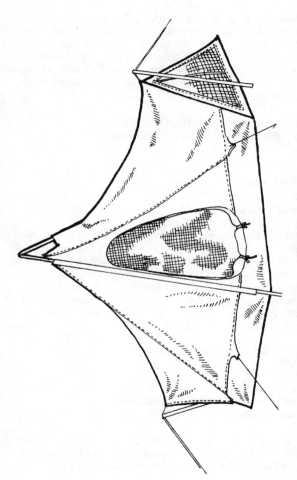

Morning Glory, by The North Face

figuration that is easy to get up. Inside space, as indicated by the dimensions above, is quite enough for the long-term base camp. Cook hole is inside door, end windows and door are vented and closable with zippered flaps. Packed in two stuff sacks so load can be shared in the party. Chosen for many Arctic-condition expeditions. Gold/taupe or gold/blue.

About $350 from North Face

RECREATIONAL EQUIPMENT INC.
1525 11th Ave.
Seattle, WA 98122

Grand Hotel
80″W x 88″L x 52″H   8 lbs. 10 oz.
Rainfly optional

A heavy-duty mountaineering tent of exceptional quality. The above dimensions do not include nearly 70 square inches of vestibule space, added to both ends. Canopy of 1.9-ounce ripstop. Coated floor extends 16 inches up sidewalls. Arch entrance on one end, tunnel on the opposite end. Three cargo pockets, cook hole in floor. Sleeve vent, doors, are fully netted; zippered storm flaps. Double A-pole supports. Blue/yellow canopy, sand floor and rainfly.

About $147 from REI
Rainfly about $53 from REI

Crestline Expedition
88″L x 60″W x 46″H   6 lbs. 6 oz.
Rainfly optional

An expedition-quality tent with vestibule and tunnel entrance. Pullout tabs for extra inside room, fully netted door and tunnel vent. Canopy is ripstop nylon, floor coated nylon extending 11 inches up sidewalls. Double A-pole supports. Comes with poles, stakes, guys, and carrying bag. Canopy red; floor, sidewalls sand. Fly red or sand.

About $108 from REI
Rainfly about $32 from REI

Crestline
88″L x 60″W x 46″H   5 lbs. 12 oz.
Rainfly optional

A 3-season version of the preceding tent, this one can be used for winter camping in moderate weather. Arched entrance is zippered, backed with netting, rear window netted and zippered. Canopy is ripstop nylon, floor and sidewalls of coated nylon taffeta. An excellent 2-person tent for most all-around hiking and camping. Double A-pole supports, side pullouts, generous sill at the front. In red, blue, or green with sand floor.

About $95 from REI
Rainfly about $25 from REI

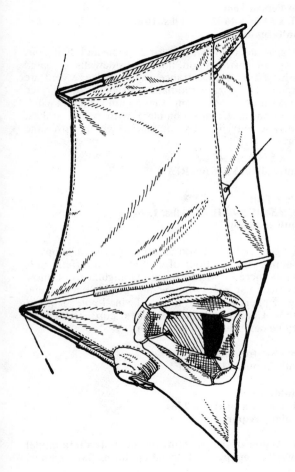

Expedition Tent

Two-Person Tent
88″L x 54″W x 46″H   4 lbs. 10 oz.
Rainfly optional

A light and compact tent for 2 people and their gear. Canopy of ripstop nylon, floor and sidewalls of coated nylon taffeta. Arch entrance and rear sleeve vent are netted and have zippered flaps. Design is sloping ridge for maximum inside room at minimum weight. Twin I-pole support. Comes complete with poles, stakes, cord, and carrying bag. In blue or green with sand floor.

About $73 from REI
Rainfly about $27 from REI

Shelter Tent
87″L x 54″W x 44″H   3 lbs. 13 oz.
Rainfly optional

A lightweight 3-season tent for 2 people. Canopy of 1.9-ounce ripstop, floor of coated nylon taffeta. Side pullouts increase inside space. Triangular front entry and triangular rear window are netting-backed and have zippered storm flaps. Twin I-pole support system. Comes with poles, stakes, cord, tighteners, carrying bag. Blue with sand floor.

About $45 from REI
Rainfly about $24 from REI

High-lite Tent
84″L x 60″W x 44″H   7 lbs.
No rainfly required

A version of the net tent, this coated taffeta model allows the canopy to be rolled up during fair weather, unrolled to cover the mosquito netting when it turns damp. Triangular entrance is backed with netting; rear sleeve vent also netted for condensation control when sides are rolled down. Solid canopy panels can be extended for shade in hot weather. Comes complete with poles, stakes, cord, and carry bag. Blue with sand floor.

About $120 from REI

Mosquito Tent
88"L x 54"W x 46"H   3 lbs. 10 oz.
Rainfly optional

A complete net tent for predominantly desert and high/dry hiking. The sloping-ridge design is exceptionally light. Floor and 9-inch sidewalls of coated nylon taffeta. Bug-free, open-air feeling in good weather. Can be covered with optional rainfly when cool or wet. Sand color.

About $63 from REI
Rainfly about $27 from REI

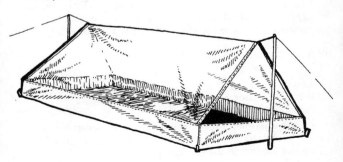

Net Tent

McKinley
78″W x 96″L x 88″H   8 lbs. 2 oz.
Rainfly optional

A pyramid tent designed for 4-person use. Ripstop nylon with coated nylon floor and 12-inch sidewalls. Entrance and tunnel vent are backed with netting. Entrance opens with vertical zipper and 2 side zippers at the bottom. Comes with pole, stakes, cord, ground pole-plate, and carry bag. Green with sand sidewalls and floor. Fly is green.

About $137 from REI
Rainfly about $47 from REI

Economy
81″L x 58″W x 41″H   4 lbs. 12 oz.
No rainfly required

A very simple and inexpensive shelter of coated nylon, suitable for basic summer camping. Floor is vinyl-nylon. Side pullouts, twin l-pole support. The entrance is of zippered netting with tie-down flaps. Zippered, netted window at rear. Not recommended for high-altitude or cold weather use. Blue or orange.

About $30 from REI

Instant Tent
9′L x 3.2′ diameter   1 lb. 4 oz.
No rainfly required

Polyethylene tube .003 inch thick. Grommets on each end to draw up opening. Green. Two-person model 4.8 feet in diameter.

About $5, 2-man about $6.50 from REI

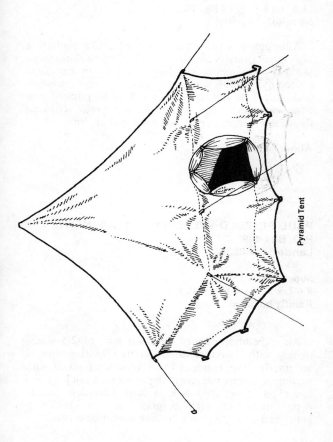

Pyramid Tent

REI Tarp
11.5′ x 13.5′   3 lbs. 10 oz.
No rainfly required

Although a tarp is hardly an adequate shelter, a high-quality tarp is an important factor (in *addition* to a shelter) in camping comfort. This is an excellent coated nylon affair with grommets all around the edges and pullout on the flat surfaces. Can be pitched in a wide variety of ways for cover, windbreak, cooking fly, or as emergency ground cover/shelter. Blue.

About $43 from REI

PAUL PETZOLD WILDERNESS EQUIPMENT
P.O. Box 489
Lander, WY 82520

Super Wand Tent
8′6″L x 5′W x 4′H   12 lbs.
Rainfly included

An expedition-quality 2-person tent of 2.5-ounce ripstop with 5.1-ounce double-coated flooring, coated taffeta fly. The entrances and vent are backed with netting and zippered storm flaps. Storage pockets and line clips inside, cook hole in floor. Complete double A-pole suspension with fiberglass wands in sides for rigidity and strength under difficult conditions. Blue.

Write for price information

Expedition
8′ 6″L x 5′W x 4′H   11 lbs.
Rainfly included

A technical expedition tent of heavy material and
fine workmanship. The canopy is 2.5-ounce ripstop,
floor of 5.1-ounce coated nylon, fly of coated nylon
taffeta. Double A-pole suspension, tunnel and triangular entrances backed with netting. Cook hole in
floor, 4 storage pockets. Catenary cut for stability in
wind. Blue.

Write for price information

Baja
8′ 6″L x 5′W x 4′H   9 lbs.
Rainfly included

Same as the Expedition model but canopies are
mosquito netting. No cook hole in floor, 2 storage
pockets. Very high-quality warm weather tent, secure
against rain with heavy-material fly in place. Blue.

Write for price information

RIVENDELL MOUNTAIN WORKS
P.O. Box 198
Victor, ID 83455

Bombshelter
97″L x 46″W x 35″H   6 lbs.
Rainfly included

An excellent, well-researched 4-season tent. The
canopy is of 1.9-ounce ripstop, the 1-piece tub floor

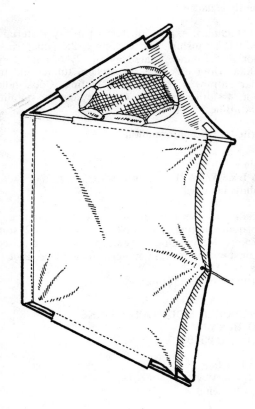

of coated 2.2-ounce nylon taffeta. Tunnel, vents, and rainfly are of coated 1.1-ounce ripstop. Double A-pole and ridgepole supports for maximum bearing and wind strength. Side pullouts for integral strength. Prow-shaped vestibule aids wind resistance. Cook hole built into floor, optional snow flaps and frost shield available. Canopy gold; floor, ends, sidewalls blue, fly taupe.

About $200. Write for price information and options. Note: These tents are not stocked; each is made (upon receipt of order) by a single worker.

SKI HUT
1615 University Ave. (P.O. Box 309)
Berkeley, CA 94701

Two-Man Mountain Tent
89"L x 56"W x 47"H   7 lbs. 9 oz.
Rainfly included

High-quality 4-season tent of 1.9-ounce ripstop, floor of coated ripstop. Net pockets inside double A-pole shelter. Tunnel entrance one end, triangular entrance other end, plus sleeve vent, all fully netted and fitted with storm flaps. Blue, green, or orange.

About $175 from Ski Hut

Fitzroy II
101"L x 56"W x 45"H   7 lbs. 2 oz.
Rainfly included

A self-supporting double A-pole design of ripstop nylon. Floor, ends, sidewalls, and fly of coated ripstop. Triangular entrance in modified vestibule end, window at rear vestibule, both netted; zippered storm flaps. Storage pocket inside. Pullouts for larger inside space. Guys not needed under normal conditions. Suitable for 4-season camping and hiking. Blue, green, or orange.

About $165 from Ski Hut

Fitzroy III
103″L x 60″W x 51″H   8 lbs. 5 oz.
Rainfly included

A superb all-season tent with double A-pole suspension, self-supporting. Frames pass through long sleeves for ease in pitching, storage pockets inside. Triangular entrance in front semivestibule, tunnel entrance at rear, plus sleeve vent. All openings netted with zippered or drawstring storm closures. Canopy of breathing nylon; floor, sidewalls, ends, and fly of coated nylon. Supports shock-corded. Very roomy for the weight. Blue, green, or orange.

About $185 from Ski Hut

Mini-Fitz
95″L x 51″W x 44.5″H   6 lbs. 3 oz.
Rainfly included

A smaller version of the Fitzroy II with the same double A-pole self-supports, shock-corded. Triangular opening in front, window at rear, both netted and zippered with storm flaps. Zippers are nylon coil. Ripstop nylon throughout; fly is zippered for secure cover, easy access. Blue.

About $135 from Ski Hut

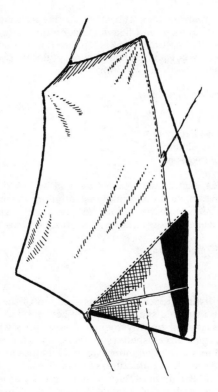

Ultimate Tube Tent, by Ski Hut

Ultimate Tube Tent
86″L x 58″W x 45″H   3 lbs. 2 oz.
No rainfly required

A far cry from the "tube tents," this modification has coated canopy and heavier coated floor. Rear entrance is solid netting; front is zippered net for access. No flaps. Twin I-pole supports with pullouts at sides. Blue or green with brown floor.

About $58 from Ski Hut

Sierra West Tarp
9′ x 10.5′   2 lbs.
No rainfly required

Another high-quality tarp that can be used as a simple shelter or to add immense comfort to the tent camp. Coated ripstop nylon with grommets around and centerline pullout tabs. With stuff sack. Dark blue.

About $32 from Ski Hut

These listings represent a cross-section of the commercially available shelters, but are certainly not all of the tents around by any means. Those who wish to look at large canvas shelters, trailers, specialized waterborne tents, or even more backpack items can write to the individual manufacturers and dealers.

Write to the manufacturers or sellers listed in the preceding catalog for current prices, new lines, or changes in material developments. They will all be happy to furnish added information upon request.

Index